Mazatlan Travel Guide
Your Go Made Easy!

MORE THAN MAZATLAN RENTALS, MAZATLAN BEACHES, AND THINGS TO DO IN MAZATLAN!

Charlie Gillingham

Special Information Page

Affiliate Disclosure

If you take action and purchase through links in this guide, I may earn some coffee money, which I promise to drink if you do. We both will have a fantastic day! Regardless, you do not pay a higher price if you purchase through this Mazatlan Travel Guide or directly from a vendor.

Facebook Page

I have created a Facebook Page to keep the information flowing about Mazatlan. Stop by to keep up to date on what I'm posting.

https://www.facebook.com/everythingmazatlan

Facebook Group

I'm creating this group, and it's a work in progress. Come by and become a member. Contribute your information and thoughts about Mazatlan, so our members are current with Everything Mazatlan.
https://www.facebook.com/groups/everythingmazatlan/

Mazatlan Travel Guide Links

Send an email to mtgyourgomadeeasy@gmail.com with "Links" in the "Subject Line" and I'll send you a complete list of links used in this guide.

Dedication

This Mazatlan Travel Guide is dedicated to all fellow travelers to Mazatlan. May your stay be as delightful as Mazatlan Spirit!

But there is one extraordinary traveler that specifically gets the top dedication. She is always by my side, and I can't image doing this traveling gig without her, my wife, and best buddy Natalie Gillingham. I know your spirit always shines! Love you, babe!

Disclaimer

The author and publisher of this book and accompanying materials have used their best effort to prepare it. The author and publisher make no representation or warranties concerning the accuracy of the subject matter covered.

They assume no responsibility for errors, inaccuracies, omissions, or any other inconsistencies herein and hereby disclaim any liability to any party for any loss, damage, or disruption caused by errors or omissions, whether such errors or omissions result from negligence, accident, or any other cause.

Acknowledgments

I want to acknowledge a few people who contributed to the information I have put in this book. For private reasons, I will only recognize them by their first names. They will know who they are, and that's what's most important to me.

Gail, thanks for the tip to register with our consulate while traveling abroad. That's very important information and is now a part of this guide. You reached out with that info in a time of need, and I thank you from the bottom of my heart.

Jim and Shari, thanks for taking us to various places in Mazatlan. It was a blast! We have an awesome connection, and I'm sure we'll be spending more time together in the future. And Jim, thanks for the information you sent me while writing this guide.

Last but certainly not least, I must thank my incredible wife, Natalie, for proofreading the draft and having the fortitude to let me do my thing. She was as important to this book getting done as I was. Thanks so much, dear!

Table Of Contents

About The Author 1

Introduction 3

Mazatlán - The Pearl of the Pacific 6

Is Mazatlan safe for Tourists and Expats? 10

Mazatlan's Three Zones, Their Areas, And Outside Areas 15

What is the cost of living in Mazatlan, Mexico? 69

Where do I live in Mazatlán? 73

Do I Need To Learn Spanish? 86

Canadian Airlines that fly direct to Mazatlan 87

United States airlines that fly direct to Mazatlan 89

Mazatlán International Airport 91

Driving to Mazatlan 96

RV Parks in Mazatlan 99

What Cruise Ships Visit Mazatlan? 102

Health Care 106

Veterinary Clinics and Grooming 111

Getting Around Mazatlan 114

Banking and ATM's 119

Insurance 123

Cafes, Restaurants, Bars, and Nightlife 124

Mazatlán Hotel Directory By Location 140

Mazatlan Annual Events 144
Mazatlan Activities 148
Mazatlan Golf Courses 151
Hiking In Mazatlan 154
Bike Riding In Mazatlan 161
Mazatlan Fishing 163
Historic Sites 168
Outdoor Adventure and Beach Relaxation 171
Resources Page 191

About The Author

Since 2008, I have been traveling each year, except in 2021, to Mexico with my beautiful wife, and this is our fourth trip to Mazatlan. I retired in 2022, so we honored that occasion by spending this winter in Mazatlan from November to the end of April.

I enjoy traveling, RVing, fishing, sports, reading, working out, and walking our dog Gracie. I love hanging out with my friends, especially my wife, our wonderful children & grandchildren, and our family!

This is my first attempt at putting a book together, and I certainly enjoyed the experience. The resources in it are convenient to have and are a huge time saver in planning and during your time in Mazatlan.

Introduction

Ok, so why write a Mazatlan Travel Guide? That's a good question because I'm not a writer! Never written a book before, but I'm giving it my best shot! I'll provide helpful information you can use from start to finish on your trip, regardless of how long you plan on being here.

Let's start with these few key things that got me started on this journey, and I'll continue from there.

- I was frustrated due to the lack of creditable online resources in Mazatlan I needed but couldn't find in Canada.
- It took way more time than needed to find a place.
- Was it in a safe area? I knew the tourist hotel areas by being here three times before, but I didn't know much about the Mazatlan residential areas.
- Was it within walking distance of all the amenities we needed?
- I didn't know anything about securing a place once I found one.
- Was the place I secured with a deposit real?
- Did I get scammed?

Everything about planning this trip, from those unknowns to seeing this place for the first time, was based on faith. Faith that I was dealing with a good person online from Mazatlan. One that I had to put all my trust into. I relied on that for my wife and I during this process. Faith, trust, and a good gut feeling!

And as faith would have it, everything worked out for us. I couldn't have asked for a better outcome, but unfortunately, I have met and heard about expats here who weren't so lucky. They got duped out of their deposit and sometimes the first month's rent and ended up with nowhere to stay. This trend seems to be rising in the minds that do that sort of thing. To help prevent that kind of thing, I am providing some solid resources that are popular with the expat community in Mazatlan.

Also, you'll get to know the areas in Mazatlan on a level that will help you decide what area best suits your budget and needs. Find a long-term rental in that area or a hotel; this guide has resources (even for your pet) to help you do that.

How about getting to know the best restaurants and bars that are very popular with expats and the areas they are located in before you leave on your trip? Or have a gander at

- the best health care options available for you and your pets
- transportation options from the airport or within the city
- Banking and ATMs
- Insurance
- Mazatlan activities
- Things to do to enjoy your vacation in Mazatlan
- Spring Break

How about fishing and golfing? Not a problem. It's covered.

From the best beaches that suit your needs to enjoying a good night of music and fun on the town, this guide has everything you need to know, from vacationing to residing here like an expat.

Your stay here in Mazatlan isn't about being frugal and shrinking your life as it is by default for so many people at home. Staying here is the opposite. It's about expanding your quality of life, often exponentially, while you slash your cost of living. I have structured three types of budgets that most expats use here. You might be surprised which one you fall into.

Your go is made easy from start to finish with many other resources in this travel guide, from flying, driving here, or just showing up on a cruise ship for the day.

To recap why I am writing this guide.

- It helps others navigate the waters at every step, from planning to enjoying your stay to the fullest, eliminating a lot of time and wonder.
- To avoid experiencing the unknowns as I did, from searching for a rental property online in Mazatlan to finding one, hoping it was legit and in a good safe neighborhood. Then having to secure it with a deposit, all without seeing it, and having to trust the person I was dealing with, whom I had never met in person.
- I get to cross off writing a book from my bucket list, and it also helps me to actualize my dreams of financial independence because it creates another income stream (maybe, lol) based on actual value exchange.

Life here feels like a dream but one I don't have to wake up from. Cheers, and enjoy!

Mazatlán - The Pearl of the Pacific

Mazatlan, where the average temperature hovers around 82° F/28° C, is a Mexican resort town along the Sea of Cortez in the southwest corner of Sinaloa. It sits at sea level, and the majestic Sierra Madre Occidental mountain range rises to its east. Those nearby mountains provide plenty of biking and hiking opportunities for outdoor adventures, and its ocean is a fishing paradise.

This city of about 500,000 people at the time of this writing offers visitors more than great weather, reasonable prices, and a stunningly beautiful location. Mazatlan is a colonial town with miles of beautiful beaches, a thriving year-round cultural scene, an abundance of fresh seafood, and a community of friendly locals blended with expats and tourists.

From the beginning of November to the end of April, tens of thousands of tourists worldwide and snowbirds come from the United States and Canada. Mazatlán is also a popular year-round tourist destination for Mexican travelers.

It is divided into three distinct zones, Old Mazatlan, Golden Zone, and New Mazatlan, with a few outlying areas like Stone Island, Playas del Sur, and Emerald Bay. Plus, three ecological reserve islands in front of the bay can be seen from most points in Mazatlan: Isla de Pajaros (bird island), Isla de Venados (deer island), and Isla de Lobos.

Each zone has its neighborhoods. Geographically speaking, Old Mazatlan is located at the peninsula's southern end, Golden Zone takes up the middle, and New Mazatlan lies in the north portion.

While Mazatlan is a fair city, most expats will live in these three zones, almost exclusively within 1km of the coast. While, of course, some families might live in the interior of the city, the vast majority do not.

Mazatlan is also home to a busy multi-purpose port located in Old Mazatlan. The terminal is connected to the east coast of Mexico and the southern zone of the United States using the Matamoros Freeway. This port's main activities are agriculture, livestock farming, fishing, mining, and cruise ships.

It has the proud status of one of the biggest shrimping ports in the world, which means you can buy fresh wild shrimp at incredible prices. They are used in many dishes in Mazatlan, such as burritos, tacos, pasta dishes, salads, and more.

With abundant tuna, marlin, mahi-mahi, swordfish, and snapper, Mazatlan is renowned for big-game sportfishing; it is big business here, and so is the solitude of fishing from the shoreline. You can spot shoreline fishermen early morning and evening, enjoying what they love to do best.

Local markets like the Mercado and the Juarez are great places to get fresh tropical fruits, fresh meat, fresh vegetables, and everything else you can think of. It has something for everyone. The Mercado is the heart and soul of downtown Mazatlan and is a favorite with locals and tourists alike. An inner-city neighborhood holds one of the most incredible markets in Mexico, the Sunday Juarez market.

Mazatlan is developing into a modern city with the ongoing construction of large condo towers along every stretch of tourist areas close to the beaches and renovations of apartment buildings and homes wherever you look. Recent renovations that have made the city even more attractive were two beautiful oceanfront parks, a wholly redone Centro Historico, an easier tourist path to El Faro (the highest lighthouse in the world) with a glass floor lookout, and the Mazatlán's Malecon, which is roughly 6 miles long (10 kms) stretching along the Pacific coastline that features high cliffs, gazebos, monuments, old buildings, and hotels.

It offers "user-friendly" healthcare, with modern, fully-equipped hospitals and many smaller neighborhood clinics. Most doctors and dentists speak English, and a standard office visit costs approximately $35 USD.

You will also find banks everywhere along the main road stretching the shoreline. There are familiar stores like Home

Depot, Walmart, and many neighborhood stores. Mazatlan is home to a recently renovated International Airport that receives direct and indirect flights from Canada, the U.S., and other international destinations.

Most expats and tourists live along the coastline, within easy walking distance of long beaches. Each part of the city has its style. Whether you're looking for a stand-alone house on a shady tree-lined street, a high-rise condo with sweeping views of the ocean and mountains, a modern home in a gated community with an award-winning golf course, or a simpler apartment or casita in a more Mexican neighborhood, Mazatlan truly has something for everyone.

So, Mazatlán is the best of all worlds by allowing you to have the vacation you want, anything from a lazy lay at the pool all day at an all-inclusive resort to shopping to eating well to full-on partying. It has sights and sounds that everyone will enjoy, regardless of age.

We have traveled to Mazatlán four times for our yearly vacation; this time, it's an extended one of 6 months. I will provide information that will make "your go easy," from planning every aspect of your trip to thoroughly enjoying your stay here to the fullest! Like finding a vacation or longer-term rental for your budget in the area that best suits your needs.

Whether you are flying, driving, or coming here for the first time on a cruise ship, there is something to help you do that. Get to know Mazatlan's insights to help you experience everything this beautiful Mexican town offers and create memories that will last for years.

Mazatlan Google Maps | Mazatlan Google Earth

Is Mazatlan safe for Tourists and Expats?

This is the number one question on people's minds considering traveling to Mazatlan, and rightly so. Mazatlan is in the state of Sinaloa, and Sinaloa does have predominant areas of tight-knit communities of Mexican cartels. Mazatlan is one of those areas. With the recent outbreak of violence in the area because of the arrest of another top cartel leader, Ovidio Guzman, for precautionary reasons, other countries have issued travel warnings, such as the United States and Canada.

Ovidio Guzman is the son of El Chapo. El Chapo was caught and arrested on the Malecon here in Mazatlan a few short years ago. So there is no doubt the cartels are highly active in this area of Mexico, which you'll have to consider if you plan to visit Mazatlan. If you are reading this, then most likely that's the case.

This is how life unfolded for us on that day. My wife and I were in Mazatlan on Jan 5, 2023, when Ovidio Guzman was captured in Culiacan, a city only a 2-hour drive away. That morning we went for a long walk from the area we were staying in, Sabalo Country, and headed north to the far end of Cerritos. We had no idea this was going on.

There was still all kinds of traffic on the move, but we did notice one odd thing; we didn't see any buses running, none at all, but we never thought about it and kept walking.

We were walking over to Cerritos to check out a few RV trailer parks in that area, and I'll talk more about RV parks later in this guide. We went into the first park we came to, and we found out about the arrest of Guzman and the advisory issued by the state of Sinaloa to stay home. But everyone we talked to was still going about their day as if nothing was happening and not too worried about it.

Except for the buses not running, everything else was still normal, lots of traffic and people walking, so we decided to go check out the next one, which wasn't too far down the road. On that stretch, Natalie pointed out the black smoke from the airport area, and again we never thought anything of it.

We checked out that other RV trailer park then flagged down a Pulmonia (an open-air taxi that looked like an oversized golf cart) and returned to our place in the early afternoon.

As the day wore into the evening and night, all businesses and bars were shut down, and the city noise level decreased to a dead silence except for the odd coo sound of pigeons. That was weird, but it was the extent of how we felt about our safety that day.

We did not see or hear about any violence in Mazatlan except for the black smoke coming from the direction of the airport earlier in the day, which was it. The next morning Mazatlan was back to normal except at the airport, where it took a few days for that to happen.

All the precautions that needed to go in place for the safety of everyone in Mazatlan happened, and I have talked with many expats here, and even Mexicans, and no one felt their lives were in danger at any time. Yes, the cartels are here doing their thing and will continue doing it as long as they can, and tourism is a big part of that business for them.

The last thing they want is to put fear into the tourist industry so tourists don't come here. Now, in saying that, you have to be wise about what areas you should hang out in Mazatlan and when unless you want to put yourself in harm's way.

So are you safe in Mazatlan? Let's see and just play along with me here for a second. Are you joining the Cartel? If your answer is yes, you are not safe. Are you leaving your resort? If you are and regardless if it's to a tourist area or on a guided tour, you are safer than in large US and Canadian cities.

If you are in a tourist area, will you get drunk out of your mind? If you are, are you going to pick fights with the cartels? If you are, you are not safe. If you aren't, you are just as safe as in the US or Canada. Do you see what I'm getting at here? The cartels will not initiate violence against you unless there is a good reason.

The irony is that most visitors to Mazatlan describe the area as safer than the area they come from, and I can attest to that, this being our 4th trip here and many, many trips to Mexico over the years. Right now, the most dangerous risk when traveling to Mazatlan is a petty crime found in most countries.

Many travelers have had to deal with the massive influx of fake news or misleading statistics regarding safety in Mazatlan in recent years. This includes sensational headlines or crime reports that don't provide the full context of the situation.

Mazatlan is a huge tourist location, and it will only get bigger. Hence, the emphasis on safety and the upkeep of security is already better than in most places in Mexico, and I'm just going to leave it at that.

Should you register with the Canadian and American Consulate or embassy when traveling outside your country?

Yes, you should. They can provide assistance and information during an emergency during your foreign travel. Registration is voluntary and costs nothing, but it should be a big part of your travel planning and security.

Benefits:

- Receive important information from the Embassy about safety conditions in your destination country, helping you make informed travel plans.
- Help both countries to contact you in an emergency, whether natural disaster, civil unrest, or family emergency.
- Help family and friends get in touch with you in an emergency.
- You are encouraged to register whether you plan a vacation or live abroad.

Registration of Canadians Abroad | Americans Smart Traveler Enrollment Program

When should I register?

The best time to register is before you leave your country, but you can also register while abroad.

What information do I have to provide?

You must provide travel information and personal details, such as your date of birth, where you will stay in the destination country or countries, and your emergency contact information.

Mazatlan's Three Zones, Their Areas, And Outside Areas

Mazatlan is a vibrant coastal city located in the Mexican state of Sinaloa. Centro Historico, Zona Dorada, and Nuevo Mazatlan are the three distinct zones. Each zone offers a unique experience, with Centro Historico being the historic heart of the city, Zona Dorada being the more modern area with many restaurants, shops, and nightlife, and Nuevo being a newer and mostly residential area. There are also tourist areas outside of these zones that I also will inform you of in this guide.

When informed tourists and expats visit Mazatlan, this information helps them determine what areas best suit their needs.

Stone Island (Isla de la Piedra)

With only coconut trees, beaches, and open-air restaurants for 14 km (8 ½ miles), the Mazatlan locals and tourists hang out in this ocean-side community with the residents. They live in beautiful new and older homes and two RV parks and have all the amenities they need for a small community. There are also a couple of tiny hotels along the beach.

Stone Island is not an island (but certainly has the vibe of one) but a peninsula at Mazatlan's most southern tip, and it can be reached by a road 15 miles from Mazatlan. Residents and tourists use a water taxi, a mere 10-minute ride to and from Stone Island.

Even though Stone Island is a small community, the area is mostly undeveloped and gives you a sense of peace and tranquility that you will fall in love with. You will never stop gazing at the beauty and wonder of the ocean, its unique islands, passing ships, marine birds, playful dolphins, and marvelous sunsets. It's simply paradise!

Stone Island is one of the most popular day trip destinations in Mazatlan. There are full to half-day excursions to Isla de la Piedra with built-in activities. Still, travelers can arrange horseback riding, snorkeling, and even mangrove visits upon arrival to Stone Island. Otherwise, Stone Island is great for collecting seashells, swimming, relaxing under palapas while enjoying fresh seafood, or sipping ice-cold beers. You can make your own way to Stone Island if you are more adventurous.

Take the Sabalo Centro Bus (Green Bus approx. MX$13 per person), and once it gets downtown, most people will get off at the Pino Suarez Market. Tell the driver you want to go to Embarcadero Playa Sur or write it down and show him. The bus will let you off across the street from where you will walk into the area where you catch the panga (small boat). It is 35 pesos for the return trip. Keep your ticket!

You will be shown which small boat to get on, and it's only a few minutes to dock on the other side. It is a 2-minute walk straight down to the beach. Return to the dock by 6 pm to catch the last boat back for the day and grab the Sabalo Centro Bus back.

Check out a tour of Stone Island

Stone Island Mazatlan Google Maps | Stone Island Mazatlan Google Earth

Playa del Sur

Playa del Sur is just to the south of Centro Historico and is essentially a residential area where you'll find newer homes than you might see downtown. It supports a local vibe with stunning ocean views from its hilly streets. Try the local cuisine, buy some of their products, listen to the stories of the locals, and get a real feel for what life in the city is truly like.

Benefits:

- A few minutes walk to all the action in Centro
- Quieter than Centro Historico
- Very close to Stone Island and its ferry
- Lots of family houses of different sizes and price points
- The locals essentially run bars, shops, and restaurants; it's an opportunity for an authentic experience
- Who like a quieter, authentic side of Mazatlan life but want to be close to the action in Centro.

Downside:

- The Playa del Sur area is near the cruise terminal, and on busy port days, it could receive lots of foot traffic to the area.
- Once, it was the place to get the best bang for your buck to buy or rent a home, but that cost is rising because of its popularity.

Playa del Sur Google Maps | Playa del Sur Google Earth

Port of Mazatlan

Mazatlán is a large bustling port city. Many goods are imported and exported through its port daily, and it has been a major hub for trade in the region for many years. There is also a car ferry to and from La Paz on the Baja peninsula. Many cruise ships visit Mazatlán each year and dock at the port. You can walk to downtown Mazatlán from the cruise ship dock, but it is probably better to take a taxi or bus.

At the entrance to the port is the El Faro Lighthouse, the 2nd highest lighthouse in the world. On the road below the lighthouse is the sport fishing fleet. There are also small boats that you can take to go to Stone Island. There aren't many restaurants or shops around the port area, so you will likely just go to/from your ship to other parts of Mazatlán.

For an awesome view of the El Faro Lighthouse and from its top a spectacular aerial view of Mazatlan and its port check out this video.

Port of Mazatlan Google Maps | Port of Mazatlan Google Earth

Downtown

Downtown Mazatlan is a vibrant and bustling area in the heart of the city. It is home to various restaurants, shops, and attractions, including the Plaza Machado, the Angela Peralta Theater, and the iconic Pino Suárez Market.

This concentrated area of shops and department stores surrounds a vast Cathedral. The Cathedral Basilica de la Immaculada Conception is the large 19th-century Catholic Church Cathedral built from 1856 to 1899 and still operates as the main Catholic Church in Mazatlan.

The Pino Suárez Market is a sizable municipal market, and it is a great place to find a variety of goods, including fresh produce, seafood, artisanal crafts, clothing, and souvenirs. There are frequent traffic jams in the afternoon because the streets are so narrow and the downtown is so busy. A few Americans and Canadians stay in this part of town. Many tours will take you to the Cathedral and Market. It is worth visiting this area to see what a Mexican city is like.

Down Town Google Maps | Down Town Google Earth

Old Mazatlan (Centro Historico)

Between Downtown Mazatlan and Olas Altas is called the Centro Historico and is referred to as the heart of the city. It is characterized by many buildings (up to 500 years old)!

It is also home to the Plaza Machado, Angela Peralta Theatre, art galleries, museums, and parks—an excellent place to people-watch and sip coffee. Centro Historico is where you should live if you want to be immersed. Many retired Americans and Canadians live in this part of town.

A visit to Mazatlan would only be complete with a visit to the Historic Old Town. This area also has unlimited trendy cafes and restaurants, endless activities and community events, and many markets and small local shops.

Benefits:

- Gorgeous architecture with stunning pastel colonial houses

- Endless activities, events, and socials
- Extremely walkable (no car needed)

Downside:

- Older homes with potential for mold, plumbing issues, etc.
- Some streets have very high levels of noise around the clock
- Potential to flood during the rainy season
- No ocean view

Take a look around the Plaza Machado.

Centro Historico Google Maps | Centro Historico Google Earth

Olas Altas

Olas Altas is the oldest part of Mazatlán, with a small bay cresting its surrounding. Olas Altas means "high waves" in Spanish. Olas Altas is the starting point for the Malecon, the city's seawall and seaside walkway, and continues for 10 kms, up to Valentino's. Across the road from the seawall are several historic hotels, restaurants, and bars with an ocean view.

The Freeman hotel is there, and its rooftop bar and heated pool are popular spots. You don't need to be staying at the hotel to enjoy it. Bring your swimsuit and cool off in the pool on a nice day. The drinks are good, but the sunset view is the showstopper. You'll have a beautiful 360 view of Old Town, the ocean, ships, and Stone Island. Take the elevator to the top floor and walk up two more floors.

I highly recommend checking this rooftop out. I must thank my friend Jim and his wife Shari for taking us there for the first time. We had a wonderful time, and the sunset was amazing!

Benefits:

- Amazing ocean views with lots of energy
- A bustling area of the Malecon filled with ocean-view restaurants and cafes
- Literal steps away from Centro Historico

Downside:

- Real Estate and rentals are reasonably priced here.
- It can be very noisy, especially during peak times and holidays

Old Altas Google Maps | Old Altas Google Earth

Playa Olas Altas

Playa Olas Altas Beach, "Beach of Big Waves," sits on the western edge of Centro Historico and is one of the most popular beaches for surfers during summer. It is also situated at the southern end of the Malecon and has been drawing tourists to Mazatlan from around the world for decades and was the first of their tourist beaches.

This beach could be better for swimming because of the waves. Still, it offers lovely views of their islands, it is especially beautiful at sunset, and it offers ideal opportunities to take a break and relax at one of the Malecon cafes while surfers entertain you! It is also lined with delightful restaurants like El Shrimp Bucket. Olas Altas beach area is still one of Mazatlan's best beaches for attracting surfers and tourists from around the globe.

But not to fret, for those who like swimming or have children who want to, there is a very cool saltwater pool, La Carpa Olivera, located at the northern end of Olas Altas beach. For decades, swimming and splashing have been a tradition for Mazatlan families and tourists. This saltwater pool is a big attraction to the area they renovated in 2014 – 2015.

For those who would like to stay at Olas Altas beach, there are classic hotels on the Malecon, including the La Siesta and the Posada Freeman, which I mentioned earlier.

Playa Olas Altas Google Maps | Playa Olas Altas Google Earth

Loma Linda

Loma Linda is the hill that overlooks the same section of Malecon, where you'll find bigger homes and estates.

Both the Loma Linda and the Olas Altas neighborhoods are located on the south end of the Malecon.

Some expats and tourists prefer to avoid living inside the picturesque streets of Centro and opt for an ocean view instead. Thankfully, you can stay in the Centro Historico area and get the best of both worlds by living in Olas Altas or Loma Linda, enjoying the ocean views, and catching the old town vibe.

Benefits:

- Amazing ocean views
- Not too far away from Centro Historico

Downside:

- Real Estate and rentals can be expensive on the hill
- It can be very noisy, especially during peak times and holidays

Loma Linda Google Maps | Loma Linda Google Earth

Los Pinos

Los Pinos is a tranquil residential neighborhood at the southern end of the beautiful bay of Mazatlán. This area is known for its peaceful atmosphere, offering residents and visitors alike the perfect place to relax and enjoy the sights and sounds of the city.

With its close proximity to the main attractions of Mazatlán, Los Pinos is an ideal home base for anyone looking to explore the city. Whether looking for a quiet place to rest or a vibrant and exciting place to explore, Los Pinos has something for everyone. It is generally a little less expensive to rent than in Olas Altas or the Golden Zone.

There are two condominium towers in operation, Boca del Cielo and Punta Bahia, with two more under construction and near completion as of this writing. Litoral Ocean Condos and Boca del Mar on Paseo Claussen are on the last area of the Malecon at the south end. Los Pinos is the area in Mazatlán where the Malecon goes from Avenida del Mar to Paseo Claussen.

Benefits:

- Quiet little area of Mazatlan
- Comfortable and Safe
- Long-term rentals available
- Non-Ocean and Ocean view properties
- Property rentals available for different size budgets
- Older to Modern Properties
- This area has all the tourist amenities

Downside:

- Construction noise and dust
- Parking Issues
- Small Beach
- Strong undercurrent and not suitable for swimming

Los Pinos Google Maps | Los Pinos Google Earth

Playa Los Pinos

One of the less visited Mazatlan beaches is located just north of the Ciencias del Mar (Marine Sciences College) and the Fisherman's Monument right on Centro. When you get to the beach, it is identified by a sign with its name. It is considered the smallest beach in the port area since it does not even reach 200 meters long.

You will see a lifeguard tower with various beach food stalls, such as coconuts and snacks to recharge your batteries. A beach umbrella vendor will rent you one for the day for a very reasonable price.

Rock formations at one end of the beach and the 31 de Marzo Fort on the other offer protection from the outside swells, making the water close to the beach an ideal place for wading and swimming. The soft brown sand and the calm shallow waves near the beach draw families here for that purpose.

But this area is also popular with shore fishermen and surfers. The outside swells challenge beginner and intermediate surfers, while the rocks provide good casting areas for the fisherman.

Most Playa Los Pinos fishermen are locals and sell their daily catch. If you drop by in the morning, you'll see what they are selling, and maybe you can even score fish-on-a-stick, one of their more delicious street foods.

Side Note: The 31 de Marzo Fort is where they keep one of the three cannons in Mazatlan that was used to defend it during the French Revolution.

Playa Los Pinos Google Maps | Playa Los Pinos Google Earth

Mazatlan Malecon

The Malecon is a long seawall that runs the length of the main bay in Mazatlan and is one of the longest seawalls in the world. There are beaches, monuments, restaurants, and cliff divers.

Many of Mazatlan's significant events, such as the Carnival and Day of the dead parades, go along its three distinct areas, Avenida del Mar, Paseo Claussen, and Olas Altas.

In the north section of the Malecon, Avenida del Mar, you will see the Monument to Family, the Pacifico Brewery monument, Pulmonia taxi monument, and the main monument in Mazatlan, the Fisherman's Monument, among others.

On the Paseo Claussen portion, the middle portion, there are many monuments such as the Continuation of life and the monument to women. The cliff divers also dive next to the Malecon at El Clavadista. This area is a popular place for families and evening strolls for the romantic.

From there, the Malecon stretches along the pacific coastline into the small bay of Olas Altas, which means "high waves" in

Spanish. This is the oldest part of Mazatlan, where historic hotels, restaurants, and bars exist.

You will see people walking, running, and bicycling from early morning to late night. If you do any of those on the Malecon during the day, wear sunscreen and a good sun hat, as it can get scorching! The best time to do those activities is early morning and evening. It is a long walk from one end to the other on the Malecon, and only a few people do it, but it can be done.

If you are not a walker, I recommend you do section walks, e.g., if you are coming from the north, the Malecon starts at Valentino's (a big white building on the cliff that looks like a castle) and walk as far as you can, maybe to the Fisherman's Monument and do the same if you are starting at the south end, as far as the El Clavadista. You can always flag a taxi or take a bus back when you tire of walking.

It is very safe, as a tourist, to walk on the Malecon. However, as with most places, incredibly late at night, watch out for yourself. My wife and I walk the Malecon, and no matter what time of the day we do, it is beautiful to take in at night, mainly because it's lit up like a Christmas tree, and it's much more fantastic for walking.

Suppose you are in the Golden Zone near the beach, e.g., at Joe's Oyster Bar. In that case, you may have a fabulous view of the Malecon at night with the lights of the Avenida del Mar, the hotels, condos, restaurants, and every other business that stretches the non-beach side of the Malecon. This is one of the best views of any bay in the world! You can also see the flashing lights of the television tower on the hill and the light from the El Faro lighthouse! Also unique to Mazatlan are the lights of the

Hacienda hotel. The hotel changes its outside lights at certain times of the year, e.g., to show a red heart on Valentine's Day and a Christmas tree at Christmas! This is one of the things that makes Mazatlan unique and special!

There are lots of large lovely condominiums along the Malecon that can be rented. They are all across the main street (Avenida del Mar) from the beach. This street is bustling and can be noisy, but it is reasonable. There are also some houses for rent in the neighborhoods behind the Malecon, which are much quieter. It is primarily locals that live in the houses in this neighborhood. Several new condominium towers are being built along the Malecon so construction noise may occur.

There are several fabulous beachside restaurants next to the Malecon that you can enjoy. These range from palapas (open-air palm-roofed structures) to full-on buildings. We have been in most of them, and every time we have enjoyed the food, drinks, service, and the beach atmosphere each brings!

MALECON SECRET: 2 tunnels pass under the Malecon and Avenida de Mar! The main one is from the Hotel De Cima to the La Corrienta restaurant on the beach. This tunnel has fantastic tile mosaics of fish that are well worth visiting! The other tunnel is not nice at all and should be avoided!

Many Canadians and Americans stay directly on every stretch of the Malecon, with more and more now living in the neighborhoods behind it.

Benefits:

- They love the breathtaking ocean views and beach access
- Can walk or bike on the Malecon for miles

- Being close to all the action and the Malecon Vibe
- If you own, you can rent it out for big bucks
- The large open area to the ocean and the sun most of the day
- Don't mind the high noise level coming from the street and construction.
- Don't mind paying the higher real estate cost and rent.

Downside:

- Want a quieter area of town
- Don't like the sun blasting at them most of the day
- Not affordable

Check out the Malecon from the eyes of a couple of drifters

Mazatlan Malecon Google Maps | Mazatlan Malecon Google Earth

Playa Marlin

Mazatlan's Playa Marlin beach fronts the Malecon along Avenida del Mar. A tunnel connects this beach with the Hotel Hacienda, and some steps lead down from the Malecon. Playa Marlin crests this sea wall for 6 km (4 miles) from Punta Cameron (Valentino's) to Punta Tiburon (south of the Fisherman's Monument).

This beach isn't recommended for swimming because of the waves, but you will see Palapas selling seafood, tacos, and cold drinks lining the way. Fishermen land their boats at the sheltered cove at the south end; a bit farther south is Playa los Pinos beach, popular with families and surfers.

Lined with beachfront restaurants, many tourists have found this a perfect area to spend an afternoon cruising the restaurants eating fresh shrimp, mahi-mahi, and coconut juice... or maybe some beer and tequila shots.

Playa Marlin Google Maps | Malecon Beaches Google Earth

Golden Zone (Zona Dorada)

The main Golden Zone ("Zona Dorada" in Spanish) only covers about one to two blocks into the city. It stretches about 2 kilometers to the north, with a main street, Avenida Camaron Sabalo running its length. It starts at the beginning of the Malecon, at the Valentino "castle" and the famous Mazatlan Letters and goes until just after "The Inn Hotel" in Sabalo Country.

This area has many beachfront and non-beachfront hotels, restaurants, bars, and shops. It is a prominent tourist zone and a favorite spot for Canadian and American expats to live and winter here. It is one of the most coveted places in town since all the buildings are relatively new compared to the colonial centro area.

These top attractions draw thousands of expats and tourists to stay there each year because of the differences in their vibe. This area is full of condos, timeshares, hotels, and long-term rentals for almost any budget. You can find cheap basic accommodations in swanky penthouses.

The Golden Zone has seen a big jump in constructing new buildings within the last few years, and that is a good or bad thing depending on whom you talk with. The good news is that more options for tourists to stay with fantastic ocean views will be available. The downside of this move to build more towers is that the amount of construction noise in the area can sometimes be overwhelming. Another is blocking the sun from vendors established in the area for years.

On the non-beach side of Avenida Camaron Sabalo is the residential area of Lomas de Mazatlan. The Gran Plaza, Stadium, and Central Park are located at the southern tip of the Golden Zone, a few blocks off the Malecon.

Benefits:

- Perfect for people without a car. Very walkable and has excellent bus routes, and it is easy to get a taxi/Uber/Didi.
- Most condos have great ocean views in this area with easy beach access.
- Tons of restaurants, from street food carts to fine dining, all steps from each other
- Beach access to two top-rated beaches

Downside:

- Loud noise from fireworks, parties, pulmonias, and tourists
- The main road Cameron Sabalo is prone to flooding during the rainy season (late June and continues through September)

- Lots of new hotels and condo buildings are under construction which gives off noise constantly, even on evenings and weekends
- Detached family homes are harder to find in this area

Golden Zone Google Maps | Golden Zone Google Maps

Playas Camaron

Two spectacular top-rated beaches crest the banks of the Golden Zone with golden brown sand. Playa Camaron to the south and Playa Las Gaviota to the north. They both have similar vibes in many ways and are often described as one extensive beach

Long considered one of the best beaches in Mazatlan, Zona Dorada's more southerly Playa Camaron is relatively narrow, particularly at high tide. The waves often break suddenly and recede strongly, usually in the afternoon. It's the perfect setup for bodysurfing, and at such times they are doing their thing and are super cool to watch.

This beach could be better for walking because of its deep sand and slope. When the tide is high, don't even bother trying! The pacific is relatively shallow for a long distance out thought, so it is suitable for swimming and boogie boarding. However, later in the afternoon, the wind picks up on most afternoons and the waves can get large, making it more difficult to swim too far.

Joe's Oyster Bar, the best beach bar in Mazatlan, is located on this beach. You can enter/leave the bar from the beach. In front of the bar is one of the busiest places on any beach in Mazatlan because you can be on the beach and listen to the music coming from the bar. If you need a jet ski, sailboat, boogie board, or umbrella, rent from Miquel directly before Joe's Oyster Bar.

And if you are into checking out the gorgeous sunsets in Mazatlan, the Playa Camaron is a perfect beach. Most days, you have an open view of the sun disappearing below the ocean, which is fantastic to watch!

Due to its prime location, the Playa Camaron area supports many hotels and vacation rentals. El Cid Castilla and Oro Beach Hotel are two popular choices in the heart of the Gold Zone and are close to an array of beachfront attractions. Plenty of restaurants, shops, and nightclubs are also geared to support the many tourists in the area.

Playas Camaron Google Maps | Playas Camaron Google Earth

Playa Las Gaviotas

Playa Las Gaviotas, which means "Seagull Beach" in English, is undoubtedly the most popular beach in Mazatlan, with all sorts of waterborne activities such as parasailing, kayaking, Hobie cats, jet skis, and more.

This beach has several prominent hotels and condos and there can be crowds of people in front of them, with less sparse crowds in other parts of the beach. This beach is wide, flat, and excellent for walking on, although a few small pointed sections disappear under the water during high tide. Those areas are still walkable, but be cautious of the rocks exposed there.

The waves on this beach are usually small, making it a fantastic beach to swim in. You will see people boogie boarding, but nobody really surfs or snorkels here. Playa Gaviotas has the same lively atmosphere as its neighbor beach, with the many bars and restaurants that line this beach, so you can kick it into gear by grabbing a bite to eat and a drink or two!

Playa Las Gaviota Google Map | Playa Las Gaviotas Google Earth

Gran Plaza / Stadium / Central Park

This area is located in the southern tip of the Golden Zone, from the Malecon to a few blocks inland near the Teodoro Mariscal Baseball Stadium. This park is intended to be Mazatlan's signature park. It is home to the Gran Plaza mall, with a casino and cinema.

It is hoped that locals and visitors will use this park for outdoor exercise! There are also lots of places to sit and relax. Many hotels, condos, and office buildings are popping up in the area, and many are still under construction.

The new Central Park is one of the most exciting projects for this area. The plan for this massive park in the middle of the city, just a block from the Malecon, is one of the most impressive things I've ever seen.

It will feature a museum, amphitheater, IMAX theater, brand new aquarium, green space, bike paths, picnic areas, ponds, pedestrian bridges, commercial space, and even boutiques.

Once this project is completed, I can only imagine the real estate values in this area!

Benefits:

- Easy walk to the Gran Plaza mall, Soriana's, Stadium, and Aquarium
- Many new options for homes, even some directly on the Malecon
- On many bus routes and central enough to not need a car
- Great area for mall walkers, sports lovers, and people who will love the future Central Park

Downside:

- Constant construction noise for the next few years
- Currently not as many real estate options as there will be in a few years
- Currently not as pretty as other Gold Zone areas

Google Maps:

Gran Plaza | Venados Baseball Stadium | Mazatlan Central Park

Google Earth:

Gran Plaza | Venados Baseball Stadium | Central Park

Lomas

Lomas is a primarily residential area behind the Golden Zone's main streets. Most homes here are larger family houses with gates, but some newer low-rise condo projects are popping up. It is a very desired area of town because of its quietness, proximity to Sharp hospital, schools, shops, safe streets, and many beautiful family homes.

Benefits:

- Great variety of homes, all situated in a quiet setting
- A very small amount of commercial shops, just enough to be convenient without being overwhelming
- Connects easily to the busy Golden Zone and Rafael Buelna. (Rafael Buelna is a world-class avenue that contains two double bicycle lanes in the middle meridian, landscaped sidewalks, and modern lighting)
- Families who want yards and quiet residential-type streets but value being outside of isolating gated communities

Downside:

- More upscale (and therefore could be an expensive) area of town
- No ocean view like in many other Golden Zone areas

Lomas Google Maps | Lomas Google Earth

El Cid

El Cid is under 'The Golden Zone' area of town but truly is its own unique neighborhood.

It is a gated community set back onto a golf course and green space, with marina access leading out onto the ocean.

The homes you will find here will range from beautiful medium-sized family homes to stately mansions. Since the community is fully walled and gated, homes aren't behind their gates and can access lots of green space.

Benefits:

- Gated and secure area for enhanced safety and peace of mind
- If you love golfing
- Beautiful landscaping and green spaces, with some houses being on the golf course or having direct marina access
- Less flooding than in other areas of the city

- Great for big families
- Luxurious living in a quiet setting
- Families with cars that love extra security, green space, and the finer side of things

Downside:

- You 100% need a car to live in this community
- It's a process to have food delivered, cabs ordered, or even visitors into El Cid
- It can feel isolating for people who like to walk to stores
- No ocean view
- One of the most expensive areas of the city

El Cid Community Google Maps | El Cid Community Google Earth

Sabalo Country

Sabalo Country is the most 'northern' part of the Golden Zone. It runs from the West gate of the 'El Cid' gated community of the town right up to the El Cid Marina Beach Hotel.

People living in Sabalo Country love how close it is to the beach and how quieter it is than the rest of the Golden Zone. Sabalo has many restaurants, shops, and bars with excellent beach access and tons of availability for affordable condos and other rental properties.

It does have a mix of hotels and condos on the beach, with Avenida Camaron Sabalo running its length. A primarily residential area on the east side of this street is filled with many Canadian and American expats.

This is where my wife and I currently reside, and we love this area of Mazatlan. This neighborhood is primarily quiet, depending on what area you live in. There are a few bars on the main drag, and if you live on the other side of the street that runs directly parallel behind those establishments, you will only regret it if you are into listening to the loud music and chatter every day.

Fortunately, we don't have that problem because it was one of my first questions when dealing with this landlord. Is the neighborhood quiet and safe? Is the building close to a bar? I guess that's three questions, but our landlord was honest with me, and it worked out for us. We couldn't have asked for a better rental, and the beach, restaurants, and bars are only minutes away, walking. The sunset is spectacular from our rooftop and the beach!

Benefits:

- Many new condos have been built recently, and many more are being developed.
- Reasonable rent prices
- Very close to the beach
- Quiet, yet still walkable to the action
- Lots of bus routes connect through Sabalo
- People who want easy beach access, a few walkable options, and a quieter scene than the heart of the Golden Zone.

Downside:

- Getting a little farther from Centro Historico and the Malecon
- The main road is known to flood during high rains
- Construction noise can be a bother in some areas of Sabalo.

Sabalo Country Google Maps | Sabalo Country Google Earth

Playa Sabalo

Playa Sabalo has long been considered one of the best beaches in Mazatlan because it is sheltered from the open ocean by its islands, Bird Island and Deer Island. It is a top-rated beach destination for swimming and water sports because of its excellent water conditions.

Sailing excursions, water skiing, parasailing, and banana-boat rides are all offered on Playa Sabalo, and the firm sand makes it perfect for long walks and checking out the views of the ocean and the islands off the coast.

It's a long and wide beach, great for hanging out, getting your tan on, and watching the beautiful sunset as it dips below the ocean to the west. There are resorts and restaurant activities along sections of this beach, with public access to it at several spots along Avenida Camaron Sabalo. I am on this beach most days walking and hanging out with Natalie and sometimes our dog Gracie! This beach does have it all, and in my mind, it is the best beach in Mazatlan by far, but in saying that, each beach in Mazatlan is known for its uniqueness and beauty!

Playa Sabalo Google Maps | Playa Sabalo Google Earth

New Mazatlan (Nuevo Mazatlan)

Almost everything you see in this area north of Sabalo is a new build. Between the strip malls and big box stores, it will feel more North American than anywhere else in the city.

Because of the large stores and its spread out, many neighborhoods are not as walkable as Centro or Golden Zone. But of course, the other side is you can enjoy newer roads, stores, restaurants, houses, and condos, which is a selling factor for some expats and tourists.

Much of the Marina area and "Nuevo Mazatlan" don't have much beach access within walking distance, except Cerritos neighborhood, which is directly on the beach. Along the miles of golden-sand beach are a dozen or so hotels, ranging from 3-star beach joints to 5-star all-inclusive and a host of beachside palapas offering up a good selection of seafood.

Nuevo Mazatlan Google Maps

The Marina

The best part about living in the Marina area is having direct access or a view of the Marina itself. You'll see yachts, sailboats, and all kinds of vessels moored from your condo or townhouse. The El Cid Marina hotel beach club is located on White Duck beach, part of Playa Cerritos beach, at its southern end. You access it by taking the water taxi from the marina port to the dock on the other side. It's only a couple-minute boat ride, and you can chill on the beach at the beach club.

This is a private beach for El Cid's guests and members; you can enjoy this quiet beach without worrying about the noise and crowds. The palapas of El Cid have good service, although the prices are exaggeratedly high!

The Marina area also has access to golf on both sides, plus it's the closest community to the new Galerias Mall and Liverpool department store. Another big draw to the Marina area is the Marina Hospital, one of the city's most excellent health facilities.

It's not the most walkable area of Mazatlán since all these new stores and hospitals are spaced out more than in Centro or the Golden Zone.

Benefits:

- Lovely marina views
- Newer condos and accommodations
- Good access to Galerias, Liverpool, and Walmart
- Short distance to Marina Hospital
- Nautical-living ex-pats and retired golfers
- Can be a beach club member

Downside:

- Not as walkable as some would like, but certainly doable
- Far from Centro
- While there are marina views, ocean views, and beach access are only present if you are a beach club member or guest.

Marina Area Google Maps | Marina Google Earth

Cerritos

Cerritos is as far north as the city currently spans. It is popular with expats because it has more economical accommodations, is a tranquil community, and has three beaches rolled into one.

While Cerritos is excellent, it's about a 20-minute drive to Centro if you plan on going there frequently. The area has a few small shops and restaurants, but only a fraction compared to the Golden Zone or Centro. The trade-off is you get friendly, quiet streets and the beach vibe of Playa Cerritos.

Benefits:

- Many oceanfront and ocean-view options are available
- Quieter than many other areas in the city
- Good beach access with a walkable beach area
- Beach bums, people who don't mind longer rides/drives, and those who value newer, more modern accommodations

Downside:

- It's far. Currently, the farthest point from the downtown Centro area
- A high concentration of expats can also result in less Mexican culture and influence on daily life
- Not many walkable options for shops and places to eat like in other parts of the city

Cerritos Google Maps | Cerritos Google Earth

Playa Cerritos

This beach has three names, Playa Brujas (Witches Beach), Playa Cerritos, and Playa Blanco (White Duck Beach). Still, it is a continuous beach roughly 5 kilometers (3 miles) long.

Although several resorts and condos have been built along this beach in recent years, it remains less crowded than many other beaches along the coastal areas of Mazatlan. It offers plenty of space and charming surroundings, like the soft white sand, beautiful blue water, palm trees, and interesting rock formations that form this beautiful shoreline.

A perfect spot in the morning to lie down, catch some sun, and soothe your soul with the ocean waves' sounds as they hit the beach. You'll soon realize that quiet stretches like this abound as you take a peaceful stroll along its shoreline. Most beaches by mid-afternoon will have live music like those found at Cerritos. One or two mariachis bands will be on the beach daily, and even beach weddings are common on this beach with live bands playing.

As many do on this beach, you can participate in traditional surfing, bodyboarding, boogie boarding, and stand-up paddle boarding. Or, if you are into sightseeing for marine life, you could see sea turtles, sea lions, dolphins, whales, and stingrays that tourists have noted to be in these waters.

Unlike the Malecon, there aren't as many restaurants on the beach, but there are a few open-air restaurants that you can check out for some local cuisine and an excellent beach drink!

The sunsets are the last wonder of Cerritos Beach at the end of the day.

As it has for millennia, the sun sets in the west, slowly getting closer to the Pacific horizon in golden hues before disappearing in a wink, gracing the sky with a colorful spectrum of blazing tangerine and fire to deep indigo blue. Occasionally sea mist or light clouds on the horizon would brush the sky in palettes of pale blue and pink blush.

Playa Brujas

Situated at the northern tip of Mazatlan, about 10 miles north of Centro Historico, this beach has big waves, and the surfers and beach bums love it. The undertow is vicious, which is why "Bruga" means "Witches" in Spanish, so caution is advised when swimming because it can be dangerous. Therefore, be careful when taking a dip in the water and ensure there's a lifeguard on duty before you go in.

Hotel Riu Emerald Bay sits on Las Brujas Beach along this stretch of the Pacific Ocean. This upscale all-inclusive hotel in a stately castle-like building is a 12-minute walk from Mazagua Mazatlan Aquatic Park and 34 km from the international airport.

Google Maps: Playa Brujas | Playa Cerritos | Playa Blanco

Google Earth: Playa Brujas | Playa Cerritos | Playa Blanco

Real Del Valle

New suburbs are popping up all over the edge of Nuevo Mazatlan. Take Real Del Valle, for example. Our Pulmonia driver Oscar took us out there to show us where he and his family lived and inform us of property for sale in this area at much lower prices than property in the main tourist area of Mazatlan.

I was very impressed; Real Del Valle is a modern residential development for families, which includes houses and condos in the northeast area close to the majestic Sierra Madre Occidental mountain range. This area includes gated communities with green spaces, pools, playgrounds, and backyards. You can pick up a two-bedroom, two bathrooms for around $85,000 U.S. or $114,000 Canadian.

This area is within walking distance of Walmart, Sam's Club, the new Galleria Mall, and the Liverpool department store.

Benefits:

- One of the cheapest places in town to buy a brand-new house, townhome, or condo within a gated community with a pool
- Not as many expats yet; mostly locals
- Close to the big box stores

Downside:

- So far out that it's impossible to live without a car
- No beach
- Not close to any restaurants or nightlife

Real Del Valle Google Maps | Real Del Valle Google Earth

Emerald Bay

It is a large bay north of Cerritos. There is only one resort, Pueblo Bonito Emerald Bay, but another is being built there. This is the most northern major resort in Mazatlan. One really good breakfast/lunch restaurant, Surf's Up, is past Emerald Bay.

Guests enjoy various activities for all ages, including yoga classes, nature preserves, botanical tours, tennis, bartending and cooking classes, Spanish classes, and creative children's activities.

It is expected that Emerald Bay will be the next area of development in Mazatlan, and new luxury homes and condos are currently being built there. Hotel Riu Emerald Bay and Mazagua water park is in the surrounding area.

Emerald Bay Google Maps | Emerald Bay Google Earth

Las Tres Islas (Three Islands)

When you come to Mazatlan, you will notice three islands in front of the coastline, and it is inevitable not to appreciate them since, from any point of the tourist area, they stand out for their greatness. Isla de Pajaros (Island of Birds), Isla de Venados (Island of Deer), and Isla de Lobos (Island of Wolves) are ecological reserves with varied ecosystems for seabirds and wild flora.

Bird and Deer Islands are the ones that receive the most tourists, and tours are in place for kayaking, snorkeling, diving, and overnight camping.

Isla de Pajaros (Island of Birds)

It has an original mix of diverse habitats, including virgin beaches, mangroves, estuaries, and mixed and coniferous forests. This diversity of ecosystems is inhabited by more than 400 species of birds, 35 of them endemic and 20 migratory that arrive from October to March. It is the first island on your right off the coast of Mazatlán. The species observed there are the white-winged pijije, the red-billed rabijunco, the brown booby, the brown pelican, the brown heron, and the blue-footed booby, among several others.

Isla de Venados (Island of Deer)

It is an Ecological Reserve in the middle of the three famous islands. On your visit, you will see different animals, such as squirrels, badgers, bats, and deer, among others, and once you are there, you must climb the mountain to admire the panoramic beauty of Mazatlan. This island is also called the Middle Island. It has a quiet beach without waves and almost feels private. When you dive into its waters, you will see abundant marine life and admire the beautiful flora.

Isla de Lobos (Island of Wolves)

Located to the left of the three islands is a rocky terrain full of cliffs, but its waters' beauty is admirably the same. At low tide hours you can walk along a small, exposed rocky beach that exposes hundreds of species of shells giving magical colors to the place.

What is the cost of living in Mazatlan, Mexico?

You can also check out the current cost of living by visiting this "Cost of Living in Mazatlan" page.

Like anywhere, your cost of living in Mazatlan will depend on your lifestyle. I will provide budgets that entail renting and not buying a property, but your lifestyle costs can be applied the same whether you own or rent here.

To justify the cost of living for all it involves, I will break it down into three categories based on a couple's experiences: the Basic Life, the Good Life, and the Luxury Life.

This will encompass every type of expat living in Mazatlan, and all monthly budgets will be in Pesos first, then converted to USD and CAD for easy comparison.

The Basic Life

The basic life is the cheapest, and for people who need to stick to a budget with no frills, live like a local scenario.

- Rent – a Mexican-style 1-2 bedroom apartment near Centro Historico. 9000 / $475 / $640
- Groceries – Fresh produce at the market and budget-minded groceries to cook at home. 2000 / $106 / $142
- Utilities – Electricity, gas, and water for a frugal couple, no A/C. 750 / $40 / $53
- Transportation – Walking and using local buses. 800 / $42 / $57

- Eating Out – Quick meals from street vendors or coffee at a café 1 to 2 times a week. 1000 / $53 / $71
- Entertainment – visit the cinema, drinks with live music in the main plaza. 800 / $42 / $57
- Cell Phone – 2 basic Telcel pay-as-you-go packages. 200 / $11 / $14

Monthly Total: 14550 Pesos / $709 USD / $1034 Canadian

The Good Life

This is the most common to expats here in Mazatlan and has a cost of living that might surprise you for an excellent quality of life.

- Rent – A newer 2-bedroom apartment or condo in a community like Playa Sur, Sabalo, Golden Zone, or Cerritos with a possible ocean view or a view blocks to the beach. 16000 / $848 / $1,135
- Groceries – From Walmart, Sam's Club, Soriana, and the local market. 8000 / $424 / $568
- Utilities – Electricity, gas, water, and internet for an average couple. 1200 / $64 / $85
- Transportation – Local bus and Uber with some walking. 1200 / $64 / $85
- Eating Out – 2 times per week, sometimes 3. A mix of restaurants, cafes, and street vendors. The occasional beer and drinks on the patio. 2500 / $132 / $177
- Entertainment – a couple of afternoons or nights out listing to some tunes, snack food, and drinks along with a couples massage or pedicure, pick up a ball game 2500 / $132 / $177

- Cell Phone – Tecel pay-go plan for two people, unlimited calling/texting, and 2GB of data each. 300 / $16 / $23
- Maid – cleaning for 3 to 4 hours once a week. 1200 / $64 / $85

Monthly Total: 30400 Pesos / $1610 USD / $2156 Canadian

The Luxury Life

A couple can live to the fullest, and then some with this budget, especially for entertainment and dining.

- Rent – You can rent a newer 2-bedroom, oceanfront condo with a pool, gym with beautiful views, and amenities. 30,000 / $1587 / $2,125
- Groceries – Shopping at Walmart, Sam's Club, Sorainas, and specialty import shops, like vegan or health food stores. 4,800 / $254 / $341
- Utilities – Electricity, gas, water, and internet. 2200 / $117 / $156
- Transportation – Gas and insurance for a car, with a few Uber / Pulmonia rides here and there. 3000 / $159 / $213
- Eating Out – Going out for meals five times a week to a mix of fine dining, restaurants, cafes, bakeries, and pubs. 7500 / $397 / $532
- Entertainment – VIP tickets to the cinema, ballet, baseball games, shopping, massages, hair, and nails, spa treatments, etc. 5000 / $354 / $265
- Cell Phone – Telcel for two people with unlimited calling, texting, social media, and 6GB of data each. 1000 / $53 / $71

- Maid – Cleaning for 3 to 4 hours, twice weekly. 2000 / $106 / $142
- Gym – 2 unlimited monthly gym passes. 800 / $43 / $57

Monthly Total: 56,300 Pesos / $3000 USD / $3985 Canadian

You now have a breakdown of the three budgets most expats use here, giving good insight for those looking forward to moving here.

Where do I live in Mazatlán?

This guide has given you enough information for you to use to determine what area of Mazatlan is best suited to you. Being a newcomer, you should know by now that most tourists and expats live along the coastline, within easy walking distance to long stretches of beach.

By asking yourself questions like the ones listed below, you should focus on your priorities and what area best suits your personality and needs.

- Does it have beach access?
- The ability to live without a car?
- Is it in the middle of all the action?
- Or do you value peace over anything else?
- What is your rental budget?
- You get the idea. Once you have this information figured out, let's move on to what you should look for in a rental property.

You get the idea. Once you have this information figured out, let's move on to what you should look for in a rental property.

What should I look for in a rental in Mazatlán?

When you are looking at a rental in Mazatlan, from your computer screen, there are several things that you need to consider, such as location, price, and the amenities provided with the rental. The number one thing to consider is the location. Is it on or close to the beach? Do you want a quiet location or more action? Is the neighborhood safe? The second thing to consider is the price.

As for amenities, air-conditioning is a requirement, even during the winter months here, because it can get hot in Mazatlan. Be sure to define what is included in the rent. For example, long-term rentals (6 months to a year) may not include utilities. So you need to ask what utilities are included.

Additionally, ensure that the rental is furnished. You don't want to show up to an empty place! In Spanish, furnished apartment is: "departmentos amueblados". See the handy rental cheat sheet a little further in this section.

Other amenities to consider in a rental are:

- air-conditioning
- furnished or unfurnished
- refrigerator(small/large)
- stove (with oven) or hotplate
- microwave
- utilities included
- hot water
- number of bedrooms
- linens included
- balcony
- patio
- Internet access
- wifi
- television
- security (deadbolt)
- washer and dryer

- maid service
- parking space
- pet friendly

Be sure to get photos of the rental from the agent to confirm that all the amenities appear as stated. Any reputable rental agent will send you photos.

Important Rental Information and How to Find One

Finding the best rentals in Mazatlan will be high on your priority list if you rent a house, apartment, or condo. Whether you want a beachfront condo with a premium ocean view or a little loft in Centro, this guide will help you navigate the process and help you find the perfect place to call home.

To recap on some things to consider for the first steps you should take in finding the perfect rental property in Mazatlan.

Budget: A place with an ocean view, you can expect to pay $1000 - $3000 + USD/mo somewhere in the neighborhood. But finding a quaint studio off the Malecon or in Centro can be rented for as little as $500 - $600 per month.

Proximity: Living on the Malecon will give you a variety of dining and drinking options and a great place to take a stroll but living in Centro or the Golden Zone (Zona Dorada), you will have almost double the options per square mile.

Lifestyle: Do you plan on eating lunch every day at one of the palapas on the beach, or do you plan on mainly hanging out with other expats in Zona Dorada? While it is easy to get around Mazatlan, finding a place to rent in the neighborhood where you primarily spend your time will make life much easier and should be a significant consideration.

If you aren't sure about the area, a popular option is to find a short-term rental first and see if the area meets your needs; you can then find a longer-term option later.

Finding A Suitable Rental Property

Finding a suitable rental property can be tricky. There needs to be a central website or MLS, like in the USA or Canada, to search for rental properties online. There are aggregator sites (list thousands of offers from trusted sites like Booking.com, Vrbo, and TripAdvisor on one site) such as Kayak, HomeToGo, or Inmuebles24 that have many options listed.

However, they need to be updated regularly. Most of the properties listed aren't usually available. The advantage of an aggregator site is that users can search from one site and compare prices. Half of the properties available to rent in Mazatlan will not be listed by an aggregate site or real estate brokerage. The owner rents many properties and is not listed or contracted to a real estate company.

For these reasons, I knocked my head against the wall while searching for a rental property in Mazatlan. I finally found one from a Facebook group which I will talk about. But, knowing what I know now through these resources, I have found that one of the best ways to find a rental property in Mazatlan, even if you have your boots on the ground, is to hire a local real estate agent.

One agent that meets those requirements is Alejandra Campos. She has access to many of these properties that aren't listed online and can work within your budget and preferences to find the perfect place.

The best part about hiring a local real estate agent to search for your new rental won't cost you a thing. Their commissions are paid by the property owner, not by the renter. She is well-known in the expat community, fluent in English and Spanish, and highly qualified to help you find your desired property. You can search her properties through this website at alejandra-campos.com.

Other Rental Agencies

Remax Pacific Life has professional's agents that are more than willing to help you find a rental property. You can take a look at all their rental listings here.

Mazatlan Rentals represents only the finest privately-owned rental homes and condos in Mazatlán's most desirable neighborhoods. Whether planning a one-week getaway, a winter-long escape, or even a one-year stay, you'll be pleased with the quality and amenities they offer on their website.

OCCAN Properties is a full-service Mazatlan real estate company offering property management services, vacation rentals, and long-term rentals for your time in Mazatlan. You can research their listing on this site.

Mazatlan Facebook Groups

You can use these few Facebook groups to research. I found this property that we are currently renting through one. It will be the first one listed below, but the others are just as good. From start to finish, all communications were good, and it helped that my landlord also spoke good English.

I got a good gut feeling from our conversations, and trust was established early. But there was still some uneasiness on my part until I got here and saw the place in person for the first time. That was a significant relief, I have to tell you, and we couldn't have asked for a better outcome. Our Landlords have gone above and beyond to fix any issues and ensure our stay here is good. Top-notch service all the way.

We had also used Mazatlán 4 Rent before on another trip and had no issues with them, and their service was also excellent.

Of course, you do have to do your due diligence. As you know, unscrupulous people are looking to take advantage of you everywhere, so you must know that can happen.

I joined these groups long before I pulled the plug on striking a deal to rent this property. My approach was to look and observe. I wanted to get a feel for the group's regular posters offering their property for rent and their commenter's comments.

This approach gave me a good sense of whom I could trust, and it worked out for me, but you do have to do your due diligence. If you find a property on Facebook and want to deal with the poster, that's entirely up to you. You do have the option to contact Alejandra Campos or any other agent. It doesn't cost you anything but peace of mind for them to look at a property for you.

Here is a list of Facebook Groups that can assist you in your search for rental properties in Mazatlan.

- **Mazatlán Area Long-Term-Rentals** Only is a group created to list easy-to-navigate LONG-TERM-RENTALS in the Mazatlan area—six months minimum.
- **Only Rentals Mazatlán** is for rental properties and home services, and you can visit it here.
- **Mazatlán Rent & Buy** is dedicated solely to Mazatlan Real Estate in English - Rentals & Houses for Sale.
- **Mazatlan4Rent** offers Mazatlán's finest selection of luxurious, affordable properties for your next vacation.
- **Mazatlan Rentals & Management** offers various properties in different areas of Mazatlan to help you enjoy your dream vacation. Book your property online quickly and safely.
- **Mazatlán Snowbird Rentals-House Sit** is a group primarily for finding those "word of mouth" rentals the annual snowbirds are looking for.
- **Landlord, Tenant, and Rental Reviews in Mazatlan** - Any landlord or renter experience with an address. Positive and negative. Ask about a landlord before you rent.

Finding The Best Rentals in Mazatlan, Like a Local

Mexico has recently seen an extreme boom in the number of people relocating from Canada and the U.S., and Mazatlan has seen its fair share.

Mainly after the pandemic because there was a surge in the number of people who either became remote workers or decided life was too short and retired early.

Now, what does this have to do with finding the best rentals? Let me explain, "Search Where The Locals Search." Time and time again, I've seen the rising costs of rentals advertised online. And it begs the question, "who are they advertising these rentals to?"

They're not for locals; they are targeting foreigners. Foreigners whose dollars afford them a higher cost of living in Mexico. Your dollars have significantly more purchasing power in Mexico. But that doesn't mean that just because you can afford it, you're not overpaying.

I want to share how to find the best rentals in Mexico. If you're looking for inexpensive rentals, you won't find them in the various ex-pat groups. These groups are not meant for locals. They are meant for English-speaking people like you to have a platform to share information.

You have to search as a local would search. That includes learning some common keywords when you start your search.

Keywords such as:

- Rentas baratas mazatlan (cheap rentals mazatlan)
- Rentas económicas mazatlan (Mazatlan economic rents)
- Departamento barato mazatlan (Mazatlan cheap apartment)
- Casas baratas en renta mazatlan (Cheap houses for rent mazatlan)

When you're looking online and only finding the most expensive rentals, you might not be looking in the right places or with the right keywords. You have to search how a local would search. Also, a good translation app can help in a crunch.

TIP: If you are searching from another country, it will also help if you have a VPN (a virtual private network) installed on your phone or computer you are using to do your search. Just set the country you are searching in; in this case, it would be Mexico and the city Mazatlan.

Handy Cheat Sheet For Renting in Mazatlan

- What's included? - Que incluye?
- Is there a washer and dryer? – Tiene lavadora y secadora?
- A 2-bedroom apartment – Departamento de dos cuandos.
- How many bathrooms? – Cantos baños?
- Is it furnished? Esta ambueblado?
- Deposit – Deposito
- Unfurnished- Sin amueblar
- Do you allow pets? – Aceptan mascotas?
- Is maintenance included? – Esta uncluido el mantenimiento?
- Co-signer - Fiador o Aval

Where Can You Find Affordable Rentals?

Word of mouth is the best way to find affordable rentals in Mazatlan. Plenty of great rentals in Mazatlan are NOT advertised online.

I also recommend Facebook groups and the Facebook marketplace. However, remember that you'll likely need to know

Spanish to speak with whoever advertises a rental. Or at least know someone who can translate for you.

If you don't know anyone, this is when having a realtor can help you find an excellent rental in Mazatlan.

Expectation vs. Reality

You may also need to be realistic with your expectations. If you must live facing an ocean-front, modern high rise you'll pay more. Or, if you want to live in one of the trendiest neighborhoods of Mazatlan, there will be more competition, and it will be harder to find the most inexpensive rentals.

Different Types of Rental Contracts

Depending on the length of your stay, numerous rental contracts exist. Remember that the longer your contract is, the better your deal will get.

Short-term contracts are preferred by expats who have recently arrived and wish to take their time looking for a home and longer-term rental or purchase. This type of contract is also used by tourists here for days to 6 months.

6-month contracts are also prevalent here in Mazatlan and preferred by snowbirds.

Long-term contracts: These are preferred by those wishing to settle down and ordinarily last at least one year.

Rental Policies for Contracts in Mazatlan

When you and the landlord have agreed on an offer, you must sign a contract or a rental agreement. To be legal, the rental contract must be in Spanish. However, most agents and landlords will also provide you with a copy in English for you to review.

Under Mexican law, you have rights as a tenant and will be guaranteed when you sign your contract, but here are some of the things to know going into a rental agreement:

Rent is paid monthly on the day you sign your contract. The most common practice is paying the first month's rent and security deposit when the contract is signed. One change would be if you are looking to rent a property a few months down the road – in that case, many owners will want the deposit upfront and allow you to sign a contract to hold the unit. You will then pay the first month's rent when you receive the keys to the unit.

At the end of the contract, the landlord has 30 days to return your deposit. They are entitled to deduct part of the deposit if there is any damage. Always make sure that you get authorization to do any sort of remodeling before proceeding.

The property owner must maintain the property in a livable condition and is responsible for any repairs needed.

The landlord and the tenant should only renew the contract once the agreement is finished; however, you must be notified at least two months in advance if one or the other intends to do so beforehand.

Both parties have the right not to renew the contract at the end of the agreement. If you opt for a month-to-month lease, either party can terminate this with a 30-day notice.

Documents Needed From Foreigners Renting In Mazatlan

The requirements and documents that the owner will ask you to rent a property will vary. Still, with many expats coming down, they usually make it easy. However, the most common ones are the following:

Proof of identity: Passport

Proof of residency: Documents issued by immigration if you are not planning on immigrating. Your tourist card (FMM) is acceptable.

Rental Deposit

When you sign your contract, you will be asked to pay the first month's rent and a deposit, usually equivalent to one month's rent. Avoid paying cash. Use bank transfers instead.

Or you will be asked to pay a deposit when you sign your contract. In most cases, your deposit amount will equal one month's rent.

If you rent a furnished property, you should inventory all of the furniture in the property and take pictures when you move in. Here in Mazatlan, we rarely hear about disagreements between renters and landlords over damage, but it is always best to protect yourself. When you move in, send the pictures to your real estate agent or landlord.

Unless it is stated differently in your agreement – your deposit must be returned within 30 days of when you move out.

Paying For Utilities

This will vary from property to property, but you should expect to pay your CFE Bill (electric) at a minimum. Most properties will include water in your rent; some will even include basic wifi.

Extras such as cable or water delivery will be extra and paid for by the renter. It is easy to pay your utilities – most utilities can be paid online or at one of the nearby Oxxos with either cash or a bank card.

Other Tidbits About Renting In Mazatlan

Remember that rental prices are usually listed in pesos, and your contract will likely be in pesos, not US or Canadian dollars. There are many properties on local search platforms such as Facebook Marketplace. However, some unscrupulous people are also looking to take advantage of you.

Contact a realtor; they will be happy to look at the property and send you a video. Just remember – *if it sounds too good to be true, it probably is!*

Do I Need To Learn Spanish?

The quick answer is yes, you should learn some basic Spanish, especially if you have just moved into Mexico or are still getting settled. As you get more comfortable, you will want to speak more of the local language as you navigate around town. Many restaurants in Mazatlan have English menus available, and many still need to.

Many locals do not speak English but have a basic knowledge and can communicate with you; however, getting to a basic level is still highly recommended – it will help your quality of life tremendously. Do you need to go to school and become fluent and conversational? No, probably not – especially if you are coming down to retire and will spend time mainly in the area frequented by expats.

Canadian Airlines that fly direct to Mazatlan

Presently three airlines fly non-stop from Canada to Mazatlan: Swoop, WestJet, and Sunwing.

Sunwing

is a seasonal chartered airline and its main business is offering all-inclusive flights and hotel vacation packages. Many travelers aren't aware that their flights can be booked separately. WestJet is in the process of buying out Sunwing, so expect some changes with this airline down the road.

They currently depart from Montreal, Toronto, Winnipeg, Calgary, Edmonton, Kelowna, and Vancouver airports, which I know of. Still, your best bet, because of the revolving door they work under, it's best to check with the closest major airport in your area to see if they offer high-season flights to Mazatlan.

Swoop

is the newest of the three; you can find low-cost flights leaving Canada to Mazatlan. Currently, they fly from Abbotsford and Edmonton.

WestJet

is a well-known carrier in Canada and they have been flying to Mazatlan for years. They try to be budget-friendly, but the one thing they consistently offer is their high standard of customer service. This is why many Canadians continue to fly with them.

They offer direct and stop flights to Mazatlan and fly from Vancouver, Calgary, Edmonton, Winnipeg, and Toronto. And again, because of this ever-evolving industry, check with your nearest major airport to see if they offer flights to Mazatlan.

United States airlines that fly direct to Mazatlan

There are currently five cities in the USA that fly directly to Mazatlan, with three of them being year-round.

Alaska Air

Alaska Air offers year-round flights from Los Angeles. Their roots are traced to 1932, a major airline in the United States that offered more flights to more destinations from the west coast than any other airline. They fly in the United States, Canada, Mexico, Costa Rica, and Belize under the Alaska Airlines and Horizon Air brands.

American Airlines

American Airlines offers year-round flights from Phoenix and Dallas. American Airlines has been stable in the industry for a long time, starting with its first flight by Charles Lindbergh on April 15, 1926, and has grown into one of the largest airlines in the world.

United Airlines

United Airlines flies from Houston to Mazatlan two times a week from January to April. Also known as United, they are a well-known international and domestic airline and presently the third-largest airline in the world.

Sun Country Airlines

Sun Country Airlines offers flights from December to April from Minneapolis. They are an ultra-low-cost passenger and cargo airline and the eleventh largest in the US by passengers.

Mazatlán International Airport

Mazatlán International Airport (MZT) is one of the leading international airports in Sinaloa, besides Culiacan International Airport (CUL). It is also a popular destination for people traveling to the western parts of Mexico.

If you are looking for a cash machine at the airport after landing in Mazatlán, you will find it on the terminal's lower level, near the baggage claim area. The ATMs are from the following banks: BBVA Bancomer, HSBC, and Bancoppel. Forgot to exchange money before your flight to Mazatlán? International Currency Exchange (ICE) is located in the main hall on the same level and is open from 9 am until 5 pm.

If you need to buy something last minute, you will find travel essentials at the Airport Market in the public hall of the terminal. You'll find some souvenirs at Mexican Souvenirs & Gifts near the market. You can also buy jewelry at María Bonita and Cielito Lindo, which are in the public hall.

People with late flights to Mazatlán may want to consider booking a room near the airport to avoid a late-night trip into the city. Estrella Del Mar Resort Mazatlán is about a 10-minute drive from the airport, and it is possible to request a shuttle ride.

Are there any restaurants at Mazatlán International Airport?

Yes, if you want to have a bite to eat, then go to Restaurant & Bar Flap's, which is in the terminal's public area and is open from 5 am to 9 pm. You can also get a burger at Carl's Jr or a pastry with a cup of coffee at Café Punta del Cielo, both in the public hall.

What if my luggage gets lost at the airport in Mazatlán?

If you lose your belongings or find a stray piece of luggage, go to the Lost and Found Department on the terminal's lower level and next to the airport ID cards office. If your checked baggage was lost, contact the respective airline directly.

Does Mazatlán International Airport provide facilities for passengers with special needs?

Yes, Mazatlán International Airport features facilities that aim to make transit through the airport easy for all passengers. The facilities include elevators, ramps, handrails, and accessible toilets. Wheelchairs and special assistance are provided at no additional costs, but it is necessary to inform the airline in advance. It is also recommended to contact the airline about any special needs before your flight to Mazatlán.

What are the transportation options at Mazatlán Airport?

If your hotel does not have a shuttle service, you can either rent a car or take a taxi from the front of the terminal. The trip into the city takes approximately 20 minutes, and there is a taxi kiosk in the arrivals area where you can buy tickets; the cost will be about 400 MXN (20 USD). Car rentals include Alamo and Europcar, located a short walk from the airport building, near the parking lot.

Round transfer airport to hotel in Mazatlán

Round trip transfer service from Mazatlan International Airport to the hotel in the hotel zone. Day of arrival: The pick-up time for the transfer will depend on the flight's arrival time. Upon arrival, please go to the airport lobby to identify the operator. The staff wears orange shirts and beige pants. Please go to them and mention your transfer reservation.

For your departure transfer, you must coordinate with the staff when they pick you up at your hotel in Mazatán. Remember that you must be at the airport two hours before check-in.

Note: The round trip transfer in shared service applies only for Hotel zones, Dorada and Emerald Bay. The service will only be provided if your lodging or destination address is within these zones or at a private address within the city. You must request private service otherwise.

Read more about round transfer from the airport to the hotel in Mazatlán

Private Airport-Hotel Transfer

Start your vacation to Mazatlan off on the right foot by pre-booking this private transfer service. Meet your driver at the Mazatlan International Airport (MZT) and get help with your luggage to your vehicle.

Then enjoy a swift and comfortable journey to your accommodation in the city center of Mazatlan.

- Avoid the hassle of waiting in long taxi lines
- Enjoy complimentary beverages on your journey
- Choose from several vehicles to suit your group size
- A private car means a personalized experience

Read more about private airport-hotel transfer here.

Mazatlan International Airport Door-to-Door - Private Arrival Transfer

Book your Private Arrival Transfer from Mazatlan International Airport (MZT) to Mazatlan hotels. Avoid the hassle of waiting in a long taxi or shared shuttle queues and use their private, door-to-door airport transfer.

Your driver will be waiting for you at a scheduled time, and you will travel comfortably to your destination.

- Meeting with a Nameplate
- We track your Flight
- Door-to-door Service
- No Hidden Charges

- Clean cars & Professional drivers

Mazatlan International Airport to Hotels - Arrival Private Transfer

How far is Mazatlán Gen Rafael Buelna Airport from Central Mazatlán?

It isn't too far away. Mazatlán Gen Rafael Buelna Airport is 10 miles from the center of Mazatlán. It is about a 20-minute drive on average, depending on traffic.

Are pets inspected at the airport?

Upon arrival, all pets will be inspected for fleas and ticks when entering Mazatlan by air. Should any parasites be found, your pet will be held at the medical office.

Any dogs or cats undergoing treatments for skin disorders should bring documentation on veterinary letterhead specifying the condition and treatment.

This Mexico Pet Passport Requirements Guide answers all questions about traveling with a pet to Mexico.

Driving to Mazatlan

There are many routes Canadians and Americans can take to cross Mexico through the Arizona and Texas borders. The highway that connects Arizona to Mazatlan is part of the CANAMEX corridor from Canada to Mexico. This corridor starts in Alberta and continues through five states: Montana, Idaho, Utah, Nevada, and Arizona. Nogales, Arizona, the southern terminus of I-19 is at West Crawford Street, adjacent to the Nogales Mariposa port of entry into Nogales, Sonora, Mexico. This highway continues south into Mexico as Mexico Federal Highway 15 to Guaymas, 389 kilometers from the U.S. border. From there, highway 15 goes southeast to Mazatlan.

The other highway currently under construction is the highly anticipated one that begins in Matamoros, Tamaulipas (on the Texas border), down through Monterrey, Torreon, and leads up to Mazatlan. Both directions will get you here efficiently, offering incredible scenic beauty and an exciting look at the dramatic contrasts of our beautiful Mexico.

Like any new country you enter, identification is essential, and Mexico is no different. When crossing the border you will be asked to identify yourself and be issued a visitor's visa that is valid for up to six months. Remember that when entering the US, Immigration services will require you to present a valid US or Canadian Passport. A deposit of USD 200 on your registered vehicle will be required. This is only to ensure that the vehicle will return with you. And do not worry - the deposit will be refunded upon your return.

This deposit can be paid in cash, but only if it is in US dollars. In the case of credit cards, customs agents prefer the use of major non-Mexican-issued credit cards. It is highly recommended that you purchase an insurance rider at the border to cover you in Mexico. Shop around on the internet and purchase when you cross. Last but not least, you must carry a valid driver's license.

The "Autopista" is Mexico's version of the turnpike. It provides a limited access environment most of the way to Mazatlan except through towns and cities. There are few loops or bypasses. The speed limits from the Autopistas range from 80 km (50 mph) to 110 km (70 mps). Stop signs are red with white octagons that say "ALTO." A handheld translator or book might come in handy.

There are toll booths along the way to pay your "Cuota." This stop can also give you a break from the journey because you'll usually find restrooms and a snack bar. Having Mexican pesos to pay the toll is best. They always give you a "Nota" (receipt) but do count your change.

Make sure you fill up your tank at reasonable intervals; in other words, half full is a good idea until you get more acquainted with these routes. "Pemex" gas stations (the only choice) are more abundant these days, but just to be safe, remember to fill up when you are in a populated area. The choices in grade are Magma or Premium. Most passenger vehicles run fine on Magma (regular). Ensure the pump is set at "0" before the attendant starts pumping. It is best to have Mexican Pesos available to pay, and once again, always ask for a "nota" along with counting your change. Some stations, not all, accept major credit cards. Gas prices in Mexico increase a couple of centavos every month to keep up with inflation.

If you are concerned about your safety and security based on the bad publicity about Mexico that is heard over the news, you need not worry. Violence for the average person in Mexico is at the same odds as in any other country in the World. Most cities in Mexico are safe, especially for foreigners.

The only issues I heard from other travelers centered around highway 15. Being a privately owned toll road, it should be well-maintained, but that is not the case. There were concerns about potholes at certain sections with travelers in 2022, and detours had to be taken because of them. Mexican government authorities have threatened to take control of highway 15 if proper maintenance is not done promptly. For now, at the time of this writing, it's a wait-and-see-what-happens approach for 2023.

Highway 15 does have regular gas stations, vending machines, and pretty clean restrooms at all toll booths. It passes through the state of Sonora and into Sinaloa, which leads from Mazatlan to Mexico City. The best recommended halfway overnight stop between Nogales, Arizona and Mazatlan is Hotel Hacienda Cazadores in Navojoa. It's on a couple of acres and it's pet friendly so lots of places to walk your dog. If needed, breakfast is available although I don't think it's included in the price for an overnight stay.

For a printable driving map and other important travel tips and information checkout mazatlanpacificpearl.com.

Nogales to Hotel Google Maps | Hotel Hacienda Cazadores Navojoa Google Earth

RV Parks in Mazatlan

King David Tours RV Parks

Stone Island (actually a peninsula) can be reached by road to two RV parks owned by King David Tours. One is much smaller than the other, called Tres Amigo RV, but they are close.

Their parks bring a family vibe with many planned activities you can partake in. It is located just below the Tropic of Cancer and is a very affordable place to spend your holiday or winter retreat. Enjoy the ideal weather from November to May, with daytime temperatures averaging around 74 F.

Mostly undeveloped, the extensive fine-packed sand beach stretches for miles as far as the eye can see and immediately transforms the hustle and bustle of city life into a pristine paradise; I love this place, and take a look for yourself on google earth.

San Fernando RV Park

San Fernando RV Park is a little place in Sabalo Country, located in the city close to all amenities. The current lot rent includes everything. Cost in USD is $40 per night, $200 per week, and $650 per month. Check google earth for location details.

Las Jaibas RV Park

Las Jaibas RV Park is located at Cerritos, known as New Mazatlan. It is a clean gated park with 132 large sites to accommodate all recreational vehicles. This park is in a good location and you can access Cerritos beach by crossing the road just outside the gate. Monthly lot rent runs from $440 to $500 USD, depending on the length of your RV. Have a look at google earth.

Punta Cerritos Trailer Park

Punta Cerritos Trailer Park is located in northern Mazatlan overlooking the ocean. The community began as an RV Park and has been transformed into individual homes by the retirees and snowbirds that live there. Of the 79 sites, only a few are available for yearly lease.

In contrast, the other sites accommodate outdoor living homes, each with a fifth-wheel, motorhome, or another type of recreational vehicle nestled inside of unique structures with palapa roofs over them for shade and protection from the weather. Check it out on google earth.

Mar-a-villas Trailer Park

Mar-a-villas Trailer Park is in Cerritos and is located beachside. An older couple owns it, and the man is the brother of the owner of Punta Cerritos. They also don't have a website, but the park is pet-friendly and in an excellent location if you want the beach. The park ground is mostly sand, and the RV's are parked close together.

We met some friendly people from Canada and the United States, and they love it there. You can contact the owner by phone at 669-269-1347 and have a look-see on google earth.

Baraka RV Park

Baraka RV Park is a small park next to the Riu Resort in Cerritos, and for a month's stay, it's 11000 pesos. It is just off the beach at Nuestra Senora 135, Cerritos Resort. You can have a look on google earth. You can reach them at 669-990-3161.

What Cruise Ships Visit Mazatlan?

Many major cruise lines offer vacations to Mazatlan, including Carnival, Disney, Holland America, Norwegian, and Princess. The major cruise lines primarily operate 1800-3000 passenger ships and smaller lines under 1000 passenger vessels.

The port provides free tram service for cruise passengers between the terminal and the city. There is also a large taxi area at the terminal for local cabs, ready to take passengers anywhere in Mazatlan.

Transportation is very easy, affordable, and safe here. You can quickly and confidently take a taxi, pulmonia, Uber, bus, or Auriga around town. To make your life easier, look at the tour section at the end of this guide for ideas you can use while in port.

Carnival Cruise Lines

Carnival Cruise Lines has frequent 7-day cruises to Mazatlan on their beautiful Carnival Miracle and Carnival Splendor. The Carnival Miracle illustrates the luxurious cruising that Carnival is known for.

This Spirit Class cruise ship was built in 2004 and manned by a crew of over 900, serving as many as 2100 passengers. These fun seven-day Mexican Riviera cruises depart from Los Angeles, California, with stops at Cabo San Lucas, Mazatlan, and Puerto Vallarta ports.

Book a Carnival Cruise vacation cruise to Mazatlan today and enjoy the adventure of one of our many recommended shore excursions! Telephone toll-free USA and Canada at 1-800-764-7419 or carnival.com for more information.

Disney Cruise Line

Disney Cruise Line is one of the essential luxury cruise lines in the world. A part of the Walt Disney Corporation, Disney Cruise Line operates four stunning ships that pay homage to the grand era of the luxury ocean liner.

Disney Cruise Line offers passengers state-of-the-art amenities, top-rated services, and Disney-exclusive activities. Each ship has restaurants, nightclubs, shops, and recreational facilities from bow to stern. Telephone toll-free USA and Canada at 1-800-951-3532 and check out their website disneycruise.disney.go.com for cruise information to Mazatlan.

Holland America Line

Holland America Cruise Line has announced several cruises to Mazatlan on two of their most luxurious cruise ships: the MS Westerdam and the MS Oosterdam.

The MS Westerdam is a Vista Class cruise ship christened in 2004, with eleven passenger decks that accommodate over 1800 passengers and a crew of 800. It returned to Mazatlan in the Fall of 2014, with a departure from Vancouver that stopped in San Diego and then down the magnificent Pacific Coast of the Americas.

The MS Oosterdam is a beautiful ship that accommodates 1,964 passengers and a crew of over 800.

Book a Holland America Line vacation cruise to Mazatlan today and enjoy the adventure of one of our many recommended shore excursions! Telephone toll-free USA and Canada 877-932-4259. Visit hollandamerica.com for details on these cruises.

Norwegian Cruise Line

Norwegian Cruise Line has committed significantly to Mazatlan vacation cruises and has scheduled visits from their finest cruise ships: the Norwegian Sun and the Norwegian Bliss.

The Norwegian Sun is a Sky Class cruise ship christened in 2001 that can accommodate nearly 2400 passengers and a crew of nearly 1,000. The Norwegian Sun first arrived in Mazatlan in the fall of 2015 on cruises that will originate in Vancouver, Canada, with opportunities for passengers to board in San Diego and other ports along the Pacific coast of the United States.

The Norwegian Jewel is a Jewel Class cruise ship christened in 2005 that can accommodate over 2300 passengers and a crew of nearly 1,100. The Norwegian Jewel first arrived in Mazatlan in the fall of 2014 on a cruise that originated in Vancouver, with opportunities for passengers to board in Los Angeles.

Book a Norwegian Cruise Line vacation cruise to Mazatlan today and enjoy the adventure of one of the many recommended shore excursions that await you! Telephone toll-free USA and Canada 866-234-7350; for more information on these cruises, you'll find at ncl.com.

Princess Cruises

Princess Cruises are currently sailing three cruise ships to Mazatlan: the Ruby Princess, Grand Princess, and the Star Princess.

The Grand Princess was the largest and most expensive cruise ship ever when she was christened in 1998 and was the flagship of Princess Cruise Lines until June 2013. At over 950 feet in length and sporting 17 decks, this floating city can accommodate up to 3,100 passengers and a crew of 1,100.

The Ruby Princess is a very large, Grand Class cruise ship, and she was the heaviest ship in the Princess fleet until the christening of the new Royal Princess that was launched in 2008. The Ruby Princess carries over 3000 passengers and 1200 crew and boasts 19 decks.

The Star Princess is also a Grand Class cruise ship built in 2002 and refurbished in 2011, and it sports 18 decks and 1301 cabins. It can accommodate over 3000 passengers and a crew of 1,100.

Book a Princess Cruise vacation to Mazatlan today and enjoy one of the recommended shore excursions! Telephone toll-free USA and Canada at 1-800-377-9383 and look at their site cruiseweb.com

Health Care

It is a topic on most people's minds when they decide to come to Mazatlan, either as a retiree spending a bunch of time here or someone taking a vacation.

I have noticed that Mazatlan is full of hospitals, clinics, and doctor's offices. You will find walk-in medical clinics in most tourist areas and doctors in most major hotels and resorts.

Three private hospitals are staffed to handle most emergencies; Sharp Hospital, Clinica del Mar, and Divina Providencia.

Others that are also equipped to deal with emergencies are The Hospital General in Colonia Juarez (a public hospital), Hospital Marina in La Marina (a public hospital), the IMSS Hospital (Social Security), and the Cruz Roja (The Red Cross). However, with these it is recommended that you call before arrival so they are prepared to receive you.

The general quality of medical care here in Mazatlán is good. Doctors have ample time to spend with their patients; most can be seen during office hours without prior appointments or the next day.

Most doctors even make house calls for about 500 pesos ($50 USD) if needed. The best way to find a good doctor is by asking for referrals around town and on local Facebook groups.

Considering Mazatlán is somewhat of a small community, all doctors have direct acquaintances with specialists or colleagues, so referrals are fast, confident, and relatively easy. Most importantly, you need not worry as most doctors are bilingual; but for the rare ones that aren't, it is recommended to take a good dictionary with a bilingual friend or use a translation app on your phone.

If you face a severe illness or need advanced technology, Mazatlán may not have the medical services needed. Some examples include organ transplants, which are uncommon in Mexico, or cancer patients requiring chemotherapy or radiation therapy. Also, please remember that psychiatric services in English are minimal.

There are two choices when dealing with a higher level of care. Some Americans and Canadians opt to purchase medevac insurance, allowing them to be air-transported to a medical facility north of the border where language and insurance coverage are more predictable. The trip back north is the most logical choice for those covered by U.S. Medicare or the Canadian Health Care Program. Others may have a practitioner here refer them to a specialist in Guadalajara or Mexico City, where they have all the necessary tools and experience that Mazatlán may lack in those cases.

The cost of medical care in Mazatlán and other parts of Mexico is quite reasonable. Usually, an office visit to a specialist in Mazatlán costs 300 - 400 pesos, the equivalent of $30 - $40 USD. For such services as plastic surgery or dental work, Mexico is known to have great work for much lower prices when comparing it to the US or Canada.

Private health insurance in Mexico is a relatively new concept. The most reliable and established company, ING Commercial America, has various plans and corresponding rates to cover medical needs in Mazatlán, Mexico, and Internationally.

Unfortunately, if you are over 65, you aren't eligible to initiate medical coverage with this company.

Other private insurance companies, such as GNP and Inbursa, have similar age restrictions, but some do not. Most private insurance companies have both deductibles and copayments and use a rate table to determine the percentage or amount of medical services they are willing to pay. It is essential to determine the approximate costs of each service and the amount the insurance will cost you to decide if that company is right for you.

I purchased our insurance for this 6-month trip from Allianz Global Assistance Travel Insurance. They were the cheapest, and the deluxe package gave us total coverage.

Another option is the IMSS, which is the health insurance offered by the Instituto Mexicano de Seguro Social (Mexican Institute of Social Security) through a complex network of hospitals and clinics operated by the federal government. It was designed to provide comprehensive health care to hard-working families and emphasizes prevention.

If you have FM-3 immigration documents, you qualify to sign up. When you sign up, you are interviewed by a doctor and may or may not undergo a medical exam. Signing up for this is under $500 per year.

This system works like an HMO. You are initially assigned to a family doctor who takes care of the basics. If you need a specialist, your doctor takes you to one. If you need x-rays, the doctor orders them for you. The system covers all diagnostic tests and medications. In this case, though, it is up to the patient to take a dictionary or learn keywords in Spanish; some doctors know English, but most don't speak it fluently.

Regardless of whether you choose private or public medical services, remember a few things:

- Keep a file or folder for all your medical information, lab results, x-rays, prescriptions, etc. most doctors don't maintain medical orders. Be sure to take the file with you to a consultation.
- Consultations are usually paid in cash (pesos) to the receptionists or the doctor.
- If planning on being in Mazatlán for longer than a short vacation, you must make a simple plan to handle a medical emergency.
- Please note if notified in advance, a doctor can make arrangements via phone, fax, or email to contact your physician in Canada or the US. Feel free to visit some of the hospitals before you finalize your plan.
- The Marina Hospital is a world-class hospital with many specialists to look after your needs. Their ambulance service will transfer you to the emergency unit at the Hospital Marina Mazatlan.
- The Cruz Roja has an excellent ambulance service staffed with trained paramedics. They respond to all emergency calls and transport you to the nearest hospital. Several private hospitals also carry their ambulances.
- 066 is the emergency phone number in Mazatlan and is the same as dialing 911 in the United States or Canada. If you need an ambulance, dialing 066 is your best option. In most cases, each responder knows how to speak English; if they don't, they will pass you on to someone who can assist you

properly. From 9am to 5pm you can call 118 4256 to speak with strictly English speaking responders for your emergency.

Veterinary Clinics and Grooming

Whether your pet is a dog or cat, getting your friend the care it needs when traveling is always important. For pet owners spending extended periods in Mazatlan or living here full time, having access to a trusted veterinarian is an absolute must. Luckily Mazatlan has several recommended veterinarians, veterinary clinics, and hospitals equipped to handle everything from routine vaccinations to x-rays, emergency pet medicine, and surgeries.

Dr. Cesar Duarte Navarro

Dr. Cesar Duarte Navarro is a veterinary medicine doctor specializing in making house calls. He speaks good English and has substantial experience with cats and dogs. Dr. Cesar is educated at the University of Juarez Durango Campus and brings compassion to his practice.

He has successfully treated countless sick pets in Mazatlan; he is widely respected and highly recommended by many members of the expat community in Mazatlan. His address is Avenida Miguel Aleman 614 / Centro, and you can call his telephone at 669-981-7072 or his cell phone at 669-108-1187.

Clinica Veterinaria K9

Clinica Veterinaria K9 – This clinic is located just off Avenida Del Mar near the Mazatlan Aquarium. This veterinary clinic provides a full range of services, from routine vaccinations and procedures to severe emergencies. As the name implies, they specialize in dogs. They also provide grooming services.

Clinic veterinarians are available 24 hours a day by calling their cell number 669-117-1743. Their Clinic phone number is 669-958-0862.

La Jungla Clinica Veterinaria

La Jungla Clinica Veterinaria is a small animal hospital providing excellent pet care in Mazatlan since 1978. Headed by small animal specialist Rafael Aguilar de Santiago, La Jungla veterinarians in Mazatlan can do x-rays, orthopedics, endoscopy, vaccines, and ultrasonic dental work.

La Jungla has two locations; the main animal hospital downtown and their grooming facility at Avenida Camaron Sabalo 310, just one-half block from the Panama restaurant in the heart of the Golden Zone. All standard pet grooming services and pet food and supplies are also available.

English is spoken, and La Jungla Clinica Veterinaria offers pick-up and delivery services per boarding. Give them a call at 669-913-1631. Their other animal hospital and grooming service are located at Colonia Palos Prietos, and you can call them at 669-981-6197.

Veterinaria del Pacifico

Veterinaria del Pacifico is a full-service veterinary clinic that can handle everything from routine vaccinations and procedures to severe emergencies. They also provide pet grooming services. They have English-speaking veterinarians and staff that are happy to help your pet. They are located at Rio Baluarte 1034, Colonia Palos Prietos, and you can call them at 669-982-6727.

Getting Around Mazatlan

When living in or vacationing in Mazatlan, many points of interest and destinations throughout the city are within walking distance, like walking through the entire Golden Zone and strolling the Malecon and Centro Historico. If you are not up to walking, there are multiple sources of transportation you can rely on, and they are all much more affordable than sources of transportation in Canada or the United States.

Pulomonias

Pulmonias are a unique form of transportation that can only be found in Mazatlan. These open-air cabs, that look like oversized golf carts and are easy to catch, can take you to almost any destination in Mazatlan, and can be found throughout the city all day and night. Riding in one is quite the adventure, with the wind flying through your hair while listening to music playing.

Taxis

The taxis here in Mazatlan are all called Eco-Taxis and are white with either red or green stripes.

Taxis, just like pulmonias, can be found at all hours throughout the city and can take you to all the main destinations. Taxis can take you to the airport, whereas pulmonias cannot.

Red Trucks

Red trucks, known as Aurigas, are pickup trucks with covered roofs and benches on either side that can fit up to 8 people. An auriga is your best option when you need transportation for more than four people. They can be found anywhere in the city but are sometimes harder to find than a pulmonia or taxi.

Public Buses

In Mazatlan public city buses provide good services and can get to just about any area you want. The buses run non-stop from 6:00 am to 10:00 pm every day and come by about every 10 minutes. There are a few marked bus stops where you will see people waiting, but for the most part, you can just stand anywhere on the street and raise your hand when you see the bus you are waiting for. On each bus, either on the top or in the window, you will see the name of the bus. Here are some of the most common buses you will see.

Sabalo Centro

It is a big green bus with air conditioning, the fare is 13 pesos, and it runs across the City from La Puntilla (in the old town) to Cerritos point (new Mazatlan). This is the bus to take if you want to go to downtown, Cathedral, Historic Center, Central Market, Theater, Lighthouse, Golden Zone, and along the seaside boulevard, the Malecón.

Cerritos Juarez

This is the bus most workers take, and the heavy hours for them are before 8:00 a.m. and at 6:00 p.m. The rest of the day is regular traffic. You will take this bus if you want to go to MEGA (grocery store), SAM'S CLUB, or the GRAN PLAZA shopping mall, and the fare is 12 pesos.

Sabalo Cocos

This is also a big green bus with air conditioning, and the fare is 12 pesos; this bus goes from downtown to the golden zone and back but goes into town; you will take this bus to Soriana's and Walmart.

Major Bus Routes and Stops

Here is a quick reference to some major routes and stops heading southbound towards Centro from the Golden Zone.

Sábalo Centro

- Aquarium
- Fisherman's Monument
- Senor Frogs
- The Mercado
- The Cathedral
- Angela Peralta Theater
- Plaza Machada
- Olas Altas

Inf. Conchi

- Central Bus Station
- Old Plaza Ley
- Plaza Las Americas Cinemas
- Red2000 Office

Cerritos Juarez

- Baseball Stadium
- Gran Plaza Shopping Mall
- Sam's Club

Urias Sábalo

- Sharp Hospital
- Office Depot
- Soriana Supermarket

Sábalo Cocos

- Sharp Hospital
- Office Depot
- Soriana
- Plaza Ley
- Walmart
- Soriana's

Playa Sur

- Olas Altas
- The Lighthouse

Want to know more about buses?

There are over 350 of them in the city and each is owned by its driver and driven along established routes set by the union, which oversees the buses. Drivers buy books of 650 tickets at a time and must issue a ticket to each passenger on the bus.

Drivers get to keep 20% of the fares, with the remaining 80% going to the union. Occasionally, a union inspector will get on the bus to confirm that each passenger has a ticket to ensure the union is getting its 80%. The driver gets around a dime for every ticket he issues.

Banking and ATM's

Whether you would like to open a bank account in Mazatlan or simply withdraw money from your Canadian or US bank account, Mazatlan has many reliable banks, including many international banks such as Scotia Bank, Banamex, HSBC, and Santander. When banking in Mazatlan, most banks have bank clerks and cashiers who speak English and can assist you.

As of recently, many banks in Mazatlan have stopped accepting and changing US and Canadian money for Pesos. Of course, there are money exchanges throughout the city, but in most cases, your best way to get Mexican Pesos is to use your Canadian or American bank card at an ATM.

Using an ATM you get an excellent exchange rate (sometimes better than the money exchanges) even though you may have to pay a small transaction fee. If you are using an American or Canadian bank card, you should notify your home bank that you plan on doing transactions while in Mazatlan so that no problems arise when using the card.

ATM's can be found throughout the city at all bank branches and major stores, such as gas stations and grocery stores. Remember that when using an ATM in Mexico, you will withdraw in Pesos, not USD or CAD.

Here's a bonus tip: when you're using an ATM in Mexico and when it asks you if you accept the conversion rate, choose "Decline". By declining their conversion rate the ATM will use your financial institution's rate, usually LOTS better.

Living Here Full Time

If you live in Mazatlan full-time, you can open a bank account at any branch. Banking here is like home regarding checking accounts, saving accounts, using debit cards, etc., although each bank's regulations vary. For more information about banking in Mexico, contact one of the below bank branches.

Bancomer

It is a full-service bank that operates throughout Mexico and has many locations within Mazatlan. Each Bancomer location has 24-hour access to ATMs.

Phone: 669-913-0154
Address: Avenida Camaron Sabalo # 333, Zona Dorada (view website for other locations)
Website: bancomer.com.mx

HSBC

HSBC is a full-service bank with 24-hour ATM accessibility and multiple locations throughout Mazatlan.

Phone: 669-916-3425
Address: Avenida Camaron Sabalo # 251, Zona Dorada (view website for other locations)
Website: hsbc.com.mx

Banorte

Banorte is also a full-service bank which, like the other above-listed banks, also has an ATM available 24/7 and on-site English-speaking staff to assist you.

Phone: 669-915-5448
Toll-free in Mexico: 01800-226-6783
Address: Avenida Camaron Sabalo Gabriel Ruiz, Zona Dorada (view website for other locations)
Website: banorte.com.mx

Banamex

Banamex is another great banking option here in Mazatlan.

Phone: 669-913-8301
Toll-free in Mexico: 01800-021-2345
Toll-free in the US and Canada: 1800-262-2639
Address: Avenida Camaron Sabalo # 424, Zona Dorada (view website for other locations)
Website: banamex.com

Santander

A global bank offering its services here in Mazatlan.

Phone: 669-914-2434
Toll-Free in Mexico: 01800-501-0000
Toll-Free in the US and Canada: 1-877-768-2265
Address: Avenida Camaron Sabalo 400-A Zona Dorado (view website for other locations)
Website: santander.com.mx

Scotiabank

Scotiabank is a global bank offering its services here in Mazatlan.

Phone: 55-5728-1900
Toll-Free in Mexico: 01800-704-5900
Toll-Free in the US and Canada: 1-800-704-5900

Address: Av. Rafael Bueina 401, El Toreo (view website for other locations)
Website: scotiabank.com.mx

Insurance

Juan F. Chong

Chong Peraza & Associates

669-982-0260

Carnaval #1612

Juan is well known by the Mazatlan expat community for their car insurance. Email him for a quote. He also sells homeowner's/renter's insurance and medical coverage. Even before you bring a vehicle into Mexico, you can arrange everything via email and a credit card. You'll get an annual reminder when payment is due. Email: juanchong@prodigy.net.mx

Mexpro.com

Mexpro.com also sells different types of Mexican insurance such as Mexico Tourist Auto Insurance, homeowner, travel, boat, and personal watercraft. The owner, Bob, at the Nogales office, says he sells US insurance for cars going into the US from Mexico.

Top Expat Insurance

Top Expat Insurance (top-expat-insurance.com) is the best website for international health insurance plans for Mazatlan & all of Mexico. They specialize in medical insurance that covers multi-country including the USA, Canada, PLUS Mexico.

Cafes, Restaurants, Bars, and Nightlife

Mazatlan has an array of cafes, restaurants, bars, and nightlife that will appeal to all individuals. There are too many to list individually, but I will tap into some of the most popular and some we have experienced.

There is a fantastic app, "**Mztourist**," you should download. It has a list of restaurants, nightlife, and everything else you need to enjoy your stay here in Mazatlan.

Most big hotels also have fabulous restaurants that l won't mention here. But I know the weekend buffet at the Hotel Playa and the eggs benedict at The Inn are very popular with tourists and the ex-pat community.

Mazatlán has many street food vendors selling hot dogs, tacos, seafood, and other foods. Most hot dog vendors are located in the Golden Zone near the nightclubs to feed all the hungry people coming out late at night! In other parts of Mazatlán, street food vendors serve tacos and seafood on the street!

Mazatlán also has its share of the big chain fast food restaurants such as Mcdonald's, Burger King, Carl Jrs', and Starbucks.

TIP: To avoid getting sick... only eat in restaurants or from street vendors that do high volume!

Popular Mazatlan Restaurants And Bars

Agatha Kitchen Bar

Agatha Kitchen Bar is an upscale Golden Zone restaurant serving lunch and dinner. It also serves premium cocktails. It is located almost across the street from the Gaviana Resort (formerly the Ramada Mazatlán and Los Sabalos)

There are both indoor and covered outdoor sections. The modern decor has a fabulous long bar and a lit inner courtyard. They have a full menu, including salads, soups, sushi, seafood, beef, pork, and desserts. From reports, the food is good!

Allegro Caffe

Allegro Caffe located in the Golden Zone, is a cafe that serves all the specialty coffees that you would expect. Excellent reviews.

Barra Al Mar

Barra Al Mar (BAM) Restaurant and Bar is a beachfront seafood restaurant and bar located in the Golden Zone and is open for lunch and dinner. It has a palapa (grass) roof and outdoor and undercover seating. They regularly have live music during the weekend afternoons.

This restaurant is hard to find. You must walk up the alley between the big Senor Frogs store and the Golden Star restaurant on Avenida Playa Gaviotas to get to it. They have a large menu that inclues ceviche, pate, agua chile, fish, shrimp, and traditional items such as tacos, empanadas, and chicharron. Excellent Reviews!

Casa 46

Casa 46 is a new upscale restaurant located on the 2nd-floor corner of the Plaza Machado, the Historic Old Town of Mazatlán that is open for dinner and lunch (in high season only).

It is located on the 2nd floor on the corner of the Plaza Machado, with its entrance on the side street. They have both an indoor and outdoor section. The outdoor section overlooks the plaza. The floors, woodwork, and hardware in Casa 46 are original to the building, built in the 1800s, so that you can enjoy its history and charm.

It has a regional Mexican cuisine with innovation. Some of the extensive menu items are confit duck enchiladas, lobster chimichanga, panucho with roasted pork, roasted beet salad, grilled rib eye, short ribs terrine, Sinaloa style barbacoa, grilled bone marrow with shrimp fitters, and chilorio and pickled octopus tostada. Excellent Reviews!

Cheers Restobar

Cheers Restobar is a bar with food in the Golden Zone. It has live music most nights and serves beers by the liter! It's frequented by a young, local crowd. Their menu includes chicken wings, tuna tostadas, boneless chicken, beef tapas, ceviche, agua chile, hamburgers, pizza, and carnd asada. Excellent Reviews!

Chili's Pepper

Chili's Pepper is a long-time beach-front restaurant in the Sabalo Country area of Mazatlán that serves breakfast, lunch, and dinner. They serve Mexican and Seafood food. We have eaten and had drinks here, with five stars for the food. The building is starting to look run down but this restaurant is in an awesome beachfront location.

Compania Minera de Panuco

Compania Minera de Panuco is a modern upscale restaurant and bar with a retro theme in the Historic Old Town. It is an indoor air-conditioned restaurant and it shares the kitchen with the Presidio, which is arguably one of Mazatlan's best restaurants, so the food is excellent.

It has large TVs showing sports and a long bar, making it less formal than the Presidio. We haven't eaten here yet, but we surely will. A few sources have told us that the food and service are excellent!

La Corriente

La Corriente is a restaurant and bar located on the beach on the Malecon in Mazatlán. It is a great place to go for lunch or late afternoon to watch the sunset.

They have some lounge chairs where you can sit, which are very comfortable. We have been here, and the food was really good, the beers were cold, and Natalie's drinks were **good!**

Diego's Beach and Grill

Diego's Beach and Grill is a restaurant and bar located right on the beach north of the Golden Zone in Mazatlán that serves breakfast, lunch, and dinner. It is mainly open-air, but they just put up a permanent roof at the back that can be enclosed and air-conditioned so you can sit in or out of the sun. They also have some tables right on the beach.

They host the all-you-can-drink Brenster's Beach Bash on Tuesday afternoons from mid-October to mid-April each year. They also have bands after the Brenster Beach Bash and on many other afternoons and evenings during the week.

We have been here a few times and enjoyed the beach vibe experience! The food and drinks were really good, and the beach bash being very popular, is still on our to-do list. If you plan on going to this beach bash, purchasing your tickets beforehand is a good idea. You have a couple of options when purchasing beach bash tickets.

El Fish Market

El Fish Market - There are 3 El Fish Market restaurants in Mazatlán: Olas Altas, Sabalo Country, and Marina. It is a seafood restaurant. The Olas Altas location is right on the main strip and has an indoor and outdoor section. On weekends there is live music at the Olas Altas location. We have eaten at the Sabalo Country and Olas Altas locations, and the food is excellent.

El Presidio Cocina de México

El Presidio Cocina de México is one of the most beautiful restaurants in Mazatlán. It is located inside the courtyard of an ancient house in the old town of Mazatlán where vines and old trees are growing. The bar is very long and spectacular. The food is very upscale and delicious, according to the reviews. We have been in this restaurant while on a walk-about in historic old town, and it's stunning on the inside and is most certainly on our to-do list.

Fat Fish Restaurant Bar and Grill

Fat Fish Restaurant Bar and Grill is primarily a Barbeque restaurant in the Sabalo Country area of Mazatlán. Although the name implies it is a seafood restaurant, and it has seafood, it is primarily known for its great BBQ Ribs.

We can testify to those fabulous ribs, fish, and chips! It's our go-to; you can't beat the price and service!

F.I.S.H.

F.I.S.H. (*Fresh International Seafood House*) is a seafood restaurant. It is located in the Golden Zone, where Mr. A's restaurant used to be. It is high-quality seafood at a mid-range price. Everyone raves about its clam chowder; so good! It has both an air-conditioned and an outside section.

On Friday and Saturday nights, a large band plays reggae music. The restaurant patio usually fills up with a younger Mexican crowd, making it feel more like an outside bar than a restaurant. Haven't been there YET!

Friends Diner

Friends Diner is a Canadian-owned restaurant and bar located in the heart of the Golden Zone. This is a "gringo" restaurant. The owner of this restaurant used to own the Saloon restaurant and bar. You will get big portions for a medium price. It is open for breakfast, lunch, and dinner, depending on the month.

The restaurant has entertainment, such as live music and karaoke, a few nights a week during the high season. They also have a few TVs on which they will show NFL, CFL, and NHL games, although the TVs could be better.

It has daily 5 pm food specials, such as Spaghetti, Pork Chops, Cabbage Rolls, Chicken Fettuccine, Lasagna, Meat Loaf, or Roast Beef. Check their Facebook page for what the daily special is. They serve Canadian Thanksgiving and Christmas dinners for those gringos that need their Turkey dinner!

Friends Diner offers free phone calls to the US and Canada for customers. They close some days during the summer and usually reopen fully in October or November each year.

Golden Star Restaurant and Sports Bar

Golden Star Restaurant and Sports Bar is a small restaurant in the middle of the Golden Zone. It caters to a more Mexican national crowd, but gringos are welcome.

They have a few screens showing sports and they like to show big boxing matches. They will regularly have banda bands perform on weekend nights.

Gus & Gus Restaurant Bar & Grill

Gus & Gus Restaurant Bar & Grill is located in the Golden Zone and is a big attraction for gringos and locals alike. A great place to go for tasting good food and drinks and just chilling during the day. At night they have bands playing, and we take in some good old rock tunes there. The food and drinks are good, and the music is even better. Worth checking out!

Joe's Oyster Bar

Joe's Oyster Bar is a beach bar in the Ramada Resort Mazatlan. They have stepped up their game concerning food. The shrimp basket is perfect! Food is served during the afternoon up to 6 pm. It is a great place to grab a cold beer, good food, and good music!

La Catrina Restaurant and Bar

La Catrina Restaurant and Bar is located in the Sabalo Country area of Mazatlán. It is an open-air restaurant that has a large bar. It primarily caters to foreign tourists but also has a largely local clientele. It has TVs that show sports such as NFL and NHL Games. It also has weekly entertainment, including karaoke, singers, rock, and country bands.

We have been to this spot several times, and another go-to for us. We love the food and entertainment, and it's an excellent place to hang out with other gringos!

Las Brochetas

Las Brochetas is a gem of a restaurant in Mazatlán. It is located just on the outskirts of the Golden Zone. It is an open-air restaurant with plastic furniture on a busy street, but with the best molcajete (stone bowl stew) and shishkabobs (brochettes) in Mazatlán!

They don't have a liquor license so you can bring your wine or beer. The meat is fabulous! This is where you will see people dressed up, bringing their wine, sitting in plastic chairs on a busy street, and enjoying the food! This place is highly recommended for the "atmosphere" and the best meat!

La Casa Country

La Casa Country in Mazatlán is a long-time steak restaurant in Mazatlán. It is located in the Sabalo Country area of Mazatlán. It is a large indoor restaurant with parking. We have not eaten there, so we cannot comment on the food or service, but it has a large Facebook following.

La Puntilla

La Puntilla is an open-air seafood restaurant on the water at the port of Mazatlán. It is a large restaurant and has really good seafood. It also has a large parking lot next to it, so it is easy to park.

La Mazatleca Restaurant

La Mazatleca Restaurant is a beachfront seafood restaurant - with a cuisine-fused seafood menu of traditional Mazatlan dishes. It is located a few blocks north of the El Cid Resort in the Sabalo Country area.

La Mona Pizza

There are three La Mona pizza locations: Marina, Downtown, and the newest location next to Punto Valentino in the Golden Zone. The location downtown is east of the cathedral and is in a cool old maritime building. This location is called 'Mona of the Shipyard' (La Mona del Astillero Centro). It has been extensively renovated and is just beautiful! We highly recommend you try out the centro location. It's a fantastic building with great live music!

Restaurant Il Mosto

Restaurant Il Mosto is located in Centro and they carry a variety of menu items like pasta, pizzas, salads, meats, and seafood. We ate there with two family members and two friends. Each couple had a different pizza and we all enjoyed our pizzas to the fullest!

The Last Drop

The Last Drop is an open-air restaurant located at Cerritos. They have weekly karaoke (Mondays and Saturdays) and bingo (Thursdays). They also have a free pool table.

Daily specials: Mon: Italian food, Tue: BBQ Ribs or Fish and Chips, Wed: Pizza 3x2, Fri: Rib Eye, Sat: Venezuelan Food, Sun: Steak and Lobster. The owner has his brand of tequila that you can try out.

Lucky B's Restaurant And Bar

Lucky B's Restaurant And Bar is an open-air bar and grill popular with tourists and the ex-pat community. They are located in the Golden Zone and offer Mexican, Fast food, Grill, Seafood, and Vegetarian options on their menu.

They have a band or a solo artist playing each afternoon and evening with various good rock and country to listen and dance to. We have been there a few times and most certainly will be again. Lucky B's is the spot for you if you enjoy good food and excellent music.

Macaws

Macaws is a small restaurant located one block from the beach at Olas Altas. They call themselves the **'Cheers of El Centro.'** They are open for breakfast (from 8 am), lunch, and dinner. They claim to have the best-fried chicken in town on Saturdays from 4 pm. Fridays are Fish and Chips night. Burgers, Wings, and Salads are available every day.

It has a few tables inside and some tables outside on the patio. It is a Canadian-owned restaurant and bar with a small boutique hotel attached. They serve comfort food and Thanksgiving and

Christmas Dinners. Some nights they have live music, and TVs for sports are popular for NHL and NFL Football games!

Mariscos Puerto Azul

Mariscos Puerto Azul is a palapa (grass-roof) seafood restaurant right on the beach in front of the Malecon directly across from Hotel Amigo. It serves fabulous seafood for a low price. In the summer of 2017 it burnt to the ground, but we are pleased to say that it has been rebuilt and is better than ever.

You can sit on the beach under tents or on a cement floor under the palapa. We have been to this place, and I had a tasty platter of coconut shrimp with a cold beer! To die for!! When we stroll on the Malecon, we usually try one of the palapa restaurants along this beach.

Mary's

Mary's is AMAZING! I was craving some good old breakfast food, and Mary's did not disappoint! I had fluffy buttermilk pancakes and a ham and egg scramble. Just what I wanted. Great food at a great price. We will be back!

This is just one review of thousands that are just like that one! A fabulous open-air place located in the Golden Zone down the street (south) across from El Cid Resorts. She serves breakfast, lunch, and dinner every day.

You won't regret going there if you want a good burger, sandwich, steak, or anything else on Mary's excellent variety menu. Mary, a Canadian, started her business in 2003 and hasn't looked back. We always go to Mary's at least a couple of times on every trip to Mazatlan, sometimes just for ice cream! Website: (marys.restaurantwebexperts.com)

Mr. Lionso

Mr. Lionso is a longtime beachfront restaurant in the Cerritos area of Mazatlán. It has a full menu. The food is excellent, according to the reviews. They have live relaxing music most evenings.

Overtime

Overtime is a longtime sports bar and restaurant in Mazatlán. It has been in a few different locations in the Golden Zone. It is now in the former location of Twisted Mamas.

They show all the main sporting events and specialize in live hard rock music shows at night. The staff is friendly and will accommodate any sport or game they can. Most of the servers speak English well. Lots of good reviews, especially about the night's live rock music!

Panama

Panama is a full-service chain restaurant in Sinaloa. It has 3 locations (Golden Zone, Downtown, and multi-cinemas) in Mazatlán. It has a full menu and a fantastic bakery to buy pastries and cakes! The locations are indoors and air-conditioned.

Panchos

Panchos has two locations, one in the Golden Zone and the other in Sabalo Country. The Golden Zone location has an extensive menu, excellent service, one of the best restaurants in

Mazatlán, outside and inside sections, a beach entrance, and ocean views.

Sabalo Country location also has an extensive menu, excellent service, and is one of best restaurants in Mazatlán. We have visited this location several times and the food is excellent! They serve their food on oversized dishes so you definitely won't be going away hungry.

Pinups Bar and Grill

Pinups Bar and Grill is a new restaurant in the Golden Zone that opened in late 2018. It shares a plaza (and bands) with Lucky B's. The food is high quality. They have some TVs where they show the big UFC, Boxing, and Mexican Soccer games.

Pura Vida

Pura Vida is a healthy restaurant located in the Golden Zone. It has a huge menu with many healthy items such as salads, wraps, and smoothies.

Roadhouse Restaurant and Sports Bar

Roadhouse Restaurant and Sports Bar is a restaurant in the Cerritos beach area of Mazatlan. It is located across from the Mayan Palace. It serves breakfast, lunch, and dinner. It has weekly entertainment such as karaoke, live music, and Mexican, Canadian, and American sports.

Shrimp Factory

Shrimp Factory is a shrimp and seafood restaurant in the heart of the Golden Zone in Mazatlán. You can buy shrimp here by the kilo!

Surf's Up Beach Cafe

Surf's Up Beach Cafe is a laid-back cafe in the Emerald Bay area of Mazatlán. It is located right on the beach. It serves fancy coffees, breakfasts (until noon), and sandwiches.

They also have regular live music during the high season.

They sell Mazatlán Venados baseball tickets, with a portion of the proceeds going to charity. More information about this promotion is on their website's 'Events' page. Surf's Up also has a booth on the food concourse at the Teodoro Mariscal Stadium. They even sell various types of poutine, Canadian food!

Topolo Mexican Restaurant and Wine Bar

Topolo Mexican Restaurant and Wine Bar is an upscale restaurant in an old building in the Historic Old Town of Mazatlán. We haven't eaten here yet but have heard the food is fantastic!

It also has a cool bar in a separate room. Some nights there is one person playing live mellow music. This restaurant closes down during the tourist off-season.

Street Food in Mazatlán

Throughout Mazatlán you will see food stands. Typically, these are on corners. In the Golden Zone, there are many hotdog stands. The larger stands sell other foods throughout the city, such as tacos and seafood. My rule for eating street food is that the place must be busy with people! This means that the food turns over and thus should be fresher!

Fast Food Chain Restaurants in Mazatlán

There are many fast-food restaurants throughout Mazatlán. Mcdonald's was probably the first foreign fast-food restaurant. There is also Burger King, Dairy Queen, KFC, Carl's Jr restaurants, and Starbucks.

Food Trucks in Mazatlán

There are two food truck parks in Mazatlán where there are a bunch of food trucks in one location that you can buy from and eat there. One is the Golden Zone, and the other is in the Marina Mazatlán area.

El Sabalo Food Park

El Sabalo Food Park has many food trucks in the Golden Zone on Avenida Camaron Sabalo, across from Burger King. This is just a bunch of food trucks and a seating area. They have live music from Fridays to Sundays at 8:30 pm. Hours: Tuesdays to Sundays, 4 pm to 12:30 am.

Pacific Park

Pacific Park is a place that has food trucks, a golf driving range, batting cages, a children's play area, pool tables, foosball tables, and other games. Located in the Marina area of Mazatlán, this place has a great family environment, live music starting at 9 pm, and good food options.

What's So Great About Mazatlan Nightlife?

Well, it's good, but it's not great. Nightlife in Mazatlan cannot compete with Mexico City or Bogota, Colombia. La rumba in Mazatlan is far better than expected in a city of 500,000+ people.

If you're looking to party in a city by the beach that hasn't been destroyed by foreign tourism, then Mazatlan might be the top spot in all of Mexico. If you are into a good party and amazing nightlife, this guy will tell you where it's happening.

nomadichustle.com/nightlife-in-mazatlan-mexico

Mazatlán Hotel Directory By Location

Malecon Hotels

- Hotel San Diego
- Jacarandas Hotel
- De Cima, Coral Island Hotel and spa
- Hotel Perlamar
- Hotel Don Pelayo Pacific Beach
- Olas Altas Inn Hotel and Spa
- Sands Arenas
- De Cima,
- Gaviana Resort
- Hotel Hacienda
- Playa Marina

Golden Zone Hotels

- Hotel Emporio Mazatlan (Beachfront)
- AV Inn Hotel
- Gaviana Resort (Beachfront)
- Hotel Playa Mazatlan (Beachfront All-inclusive)
- Ocean View Beach Hotel
- Las Flores Beach Resort (Beachfront)
- Holiday Inn Resort Mazatlan (Beachfront)
- Royal Villas
- Hotel Azteca Inn (small hotel)
- Hotel San Diego (small clean low-budget hotel)
- Mariana Beach Apartments and Hotel
- Costa De Oro Beach Hotel (Beachfront)

- The Inn at Mazatlan (Beachfront, timeshare hotel)
- Best Western Posada Freeman - Golden Zone
- El Cid Moro Beach (All-inclusive)
- El Cid Castilla (All-inclusive)

Sabalo Country Hotels

- The Local
- Blue Pacific Hotel-Suites
- Pacific Palace Beach Tower Hotel
- Pueblo Bonito Mazatlán Beach
- Luna Palace Hotel and Suites
- Oceano Palace
- Hotel Mission Mazatlán
- Quijote Inn
- The Palms Resort of Mazatlán

Marina Mazatlan Hotels

- El Cid Marina Hotel
- Isla Mazatlán Golden Resort

Cerritos Hotels

- Hacienda Blue Bay
- Torrenza
- Park Royal Mazatlán
- Jonathon Boutique Hotel
- Villas El Rancho Green Resort
- Park Inn
- Torres Mazatlán Resort
- Marina del Rey Beach Club

- Mayan Palace
- Cerritos Resort
- Costa Bonita Condominiums and Beach Resort
- Riu Emerald Bay (Beachfront All-inclusive)

Emerald Bay Hotels

- Pueblo Bonito Emerald Bay
- Hotel Encanto Bahia Boutique Resort
- El Sol la Vida Boutique Resort and Cafe
- El Sol La Vida Beachfront Resort

Olas Altas Hotels

- Hotel Belmar
- La Siesta Hotel
- Best Western Posada Freeman-Olas Altas
- Casa Lucila Boutique Hotel

Historic Old Town Hotels

- Hotel Machado
- The Jonathon Boutique Hotel
- The Inn at Centro Historico

Pet-Friendly Hotels

- Isla Venados Renta Vacacional (Sabalo Country)
- Casa de Leyendas (Centro Histórico)
- Apartamentos Torre II Condominios (Sabalo Country)
- Wandering Monkey Guesthouse (Lomas)
- The Inn at Mazatlan Resort & Spa (Sabalo)
- Hotel Ibis Mazatlán Marina (Marina)

- Loft Sabalo (Sabalo)
- Bungalows Mar- Sol (Sabalo)
- Courtyard by Marriott Mazatlan Beach Resort (Golden Zone)
- Margaritas Hotel and Tennis Club (Sabalo)
- The Jonathon Boutique Hotel (Centro Historico)
- Coral Island Beach View Hotel (Lomas De Mar)
- Hotel Mission (Sabalo)
- Vistamar Hotel & Bungalows (Golden Zone)
- Best Western Posada Freeman (Centro Historico)
- Quality Inn Mazatlán (Golden Zone)
- Hostal María (El Dorado)
- Villa Serena Mazatlán Rentas Vacacionales (Golden Zone)
- Hotel Hacienda Blue Bay (Cerritos)
- Mariana Beach Apartments and Hotel (Golden Zone)
- Isla Mazatlán Residence Club (Marina)
- Plaza Rio Hotel (Centro Historico)
- Aguamarina Talismán (Lomas De Mar)
- Hotel Perla Mazatlan (Centro Historico)
- Hotel Posada del Parque Mazatlan (Centro Historico)
- Posada San Martin (Av De La Gaviotas)
- Hotel Morales Inn (Centro Historico)
- Kiko Hotel (Av Gabriel Leyv
- Bungalows Mar- Sol (Sabalo Country)

Mazatlan Annual Events

As a tourist or resident of Mazatlán, many events happen in Mazatlán that you can attend whether you speak Spanish or not. Attending some of these events can make your time in Mazatlán more enjoyable and memorable.

Carnival

It is the biggest annual event of the year in Mazatlán. It is more like a festival with many events, including huge parades, concerts, and fireworks. Usually, hundreds of thousands of people come out to watch the events.

This year, 2023, the Carnival started on February 16 and ended on the 22nd, and reports of over a million people flocked to Mazatlan for that time, tripling in size.

In Spanish, "Carnaval" is a Christian celebration before Lent. It runs from a Thursday to Tuesday, and Tuesday is significant in the Catholic religion because it is the last day of feasting before Lent begins on Ash Wednesday.

It is the third largest Carnival in the world, and it is the same as the Mardi Gras, but with a very Mexican artistic flavor, so lots of partying. This year was the 125th anniversary of its humble beginning in 1898!

Carnival Fair

The Carnival Fair, with over 40 rides, takes place at the same time as the Carnival. I believe this fair will eventually find its home at Central Park, but with its ongoing construction, it will be located at the Sam's Club parking lot of Rafael Buelna.

Spring Break

This happens in Mazatlan from January through April because different schools have different spring breaks, but it usually peaks in March. Many American and Canadian students come to Mazatlan to the party, being you only have to be 18 to drink here, and relatively inexpensive to do so legally.

This event is not what it used to be 20 years ago when tens of thousands of spring breakers descended on Mazatlan, but it still happens, just not as many. Most of them stick to the Golden zone and Sabalo areas of town.

There are tour packages to six hotel resorts from breaknow.com to spring breakers: El Cid Mega Resort, El Cid Marina, Oceano Palace Beach Hotel, Playa Mazatlan Beach Hotel, Pueblo Bonita Beach Resort, and Riu Emerald Bay.

If you want to stay in a more tourist area where you can leave your resort, then El Cid Mega Resort and Hotel Playa Mazatlan are all-inclusive and probably better choices. Joe's Oyster Bar is next to Playa Mazatlan and is one of the best bars in Mazatlan. The Oceano Palace Beach is also good because many restaurants and bars are nearby. The other two resorts are more upscale and not ideal for parties.

Easter Week (Holy Week)

The week before Easter Sunday, everyone in Mexico celebrates Easter and it is pretty hectic in Mazatlan. The population almost doubles with people visiting their relatives, and every hotel in the city will be filled.

If you don't like crowds and traffic, this may not be a good time to visit Mazatlan. You will experience large lineups at restaurants and bars; the beaches are jam-packed.

Many festivals are happening during this time, and "Mazatlan Fest" put on by the city is a 3-day event of beach parties, music concerts, and a parade down the Malecon.

International Motorcycle Week

This annual event takes place a week after Easter. Thousands of motorcycle enthusiasts from Canada, the United States, Mexico, and other countries ride to Mazatlan to enjoy the weather and many associated events.

There are organized events such as concerts, beach parties, freestyle shows, regional tours, stunt ride competitions, tattoo competitions, bikini competitions, and after-hours parties.

Mexican Independence Day

This event happens every September 16 all over Mexico, and Mazatlan is no exception. The biggest celebration happens the night before at the Plaza Republica downtown. It usually starts around 6 pm and goes on until late morning.

There is music to listen to, and at midnight everyone does the "El Grito" call, representing the "Grito de Dolores" call to arms that started the Mexican revolution.

Mazatlan Activities

Mazatlan, being far more than a beach resort city, does have many things and activities you can do besides drinking, eating, and dancing.

If you are into sports, they have three professional sports teams: baseball, basketball, and football (soccer). With a population of over 500,000, many more complexes and venues are here for your enjoyment.

Venados Baseball Team

The Venados play out of the Teodoro Mariscal Baseball Stadium in the Mexican Pacific League. They play from October to December, with playoffs in January. The teams are mainly Mexican players, with an allowance of a few foreign players per team. They have nine championships since entering the league and two in the Caribbean Series.

It is a lot of fun going to a baseball game in Mazatlan. Natalie and I took in a playoff game in January and had a blast. Many activities were going on, like cheerleaders doing their thing on the field, and Venny, their team mascot, was hilarious doing his act on the field. Also, the giant screen does the kiss cam and shows people in the crowd.

Plus, the baseball was top-notch. Being a playoff game, the fans were really into their team, especially when it went into extra innings. Unfortunately, the Venados team lost that game, but we enjoyed it to the fullest, as did many foreign residents with season tickets.

Venados Basketball Team

The Mazatlán Venados Basketball team plays in the Lobo Dome at the University of Durango Mazatlan Campus (Universidad Autónoma de Durango Campus Mazatlán). This is just off of Avenida Rafael Buelna, just past Sharp's Hospital behind the Honda Pacific auto dealership.

They play in the Pacific Coast Basketball Circuit, a small league from April to mid-June, with playoffs afterward. Originally the basketball team was called the Nauticos, but the Mazatlán Venados Baseball team owners purchased it after the 2018 season. From then on, they were called Venados.

Mazatlan Futbol Soccer Club

The Futbol Club is a Mexican professional football team based in Mazatlan, Sinaloa. They currently compete in the Liga MX League. The club was established in June 2020, and they play out of a new impressive 25000-seat capacity stadium, "Estadio de Mazatlan." The stadium looks like a sea monster coming out of the ground, so it is frequently referred to as "The Kraken"!

Alberca Olimpica

You will love this Olympic size pool if you are into swimming. With a length of 50 meters by 20 meters wide and nine lanes, it is used for hosting international events and improving the development of swimmers in Mazatlan and the state of Sinaloa.

Parque Lineal Hector Pena Tamayo

This park was created for sports activities. You will find tennis, basketball, soccer, and baseball fields, a skate park, and an inclusive gym overlooking Central Park.

Centro De Usos Múltiples

This sports complex has a capacity for 7000 people and houses many venues, such as boxing and martial arts, as well as cultural events and concerts.

Mazatlan Golf Courses

There are four golf courses in Mazatlan of various quality and sizes. Three courses are mainly for tourists and foreign residents; the other is a local city course. Those four courses are Estrella del Mar, El Cid, Marina Mazatlan, and Campestre. There is also a new driving range called Pacific Golf Centre and Driving Range.

Estrella Del Mar

This course is the best one in Mazatlan. It is located in the Estrella Del Mar golf condo and beach resort on Stone Island, a thirty-minute drive from the airport. It is an 18-hole, par 72 championship golf course right on the ocean, designed by renowned golf course designer Robert Trent Jones Jr., and six of the greens are right next to the ocean. This course regularly hosts PGA Latin Tour America events, and you should check out their Estrella Del Mar Golf Course website to book a Tee time.

El Cid Golf Courses

The El Cid golf course is the established PGA-rated 27-hole golf course in the Golden Zone. It has three 9-hole golf courses: Marina, Moro, and Castilla.

The original course is 18 holes which are made up of the 9-hole Moro course and the 9-hole Castilla course. Then they added the

Marina Course, a 9-hole, par 36, 2243-3457 yard course that golf legend Lee Trevino designed in 1999.

There is also a driving range and putting/chipping green to practice on.

- The Marina Course is a 9-hole, par 36, 2243-3457 yard course and is considered the most scenic of the courses.
- The Moro Course is a 9-hole, par 36, 2352-3423 yard course. This is a more challenging course. The 8th hole is called the 'Monster' and is a 611-yard par five hole!
- The Castilla Course is a 9-hole, par 36, 2230-3200 yard course. This is a more forgiving nine holes.

Marina Mazatlan Golf Course

Is the newest (2009) golf course in Mazatlán. It is an 18-hole, par 72, 5307-6747 yard golf course designed by well-known designer David Fleming. There is also a driving range and practice putting greens. There are also cars for rent and you can rent clubs at the pro shop. There is a food and beverage snack bar service available on the course.

Club Campestre Golf Course

The Club Campestre Golf Course is a 9-hole, par 73, 6597-yard city golf course. It is an older golf course. No golf carts are available at this course, but caddies are available. This is the least expensive course to play in Mazatlán. It is located behind the port in residential areas.

Pacific Golf Centre and Driving Range

The Pacific Food Truck Park and Golf have a driving range located in Marina Mazatlan. It also has a batting cage and a sports bar called Mulligans.

Hiking In Mazatlan

Looking for the best hiking trails in Mazatlán? Explore one of many easy hiking trails in Mazatlán or discover kid-friendly routes for your next family trip. Check out some trails with historic sites or adventure through the natural areas surrounding Mazatlán that are perfect for hikers and outdoor enthusiasts at any skill level.

El Faro Lighthouse

One of Mazatlan's most prominent and famous landmarks, the El Faro Lighthouse, is a popular spot and the hike to the top takes about 30 minutes. It is a fairly steep climb from the bottom of the hill to the top, with the first half being a crushed gravel trail and the top half being numbered steps, 300 to be exact. The best time to go is in the morning before it gets too hot, and I highly recommend you bring your water bottle.

At the top, there is a glass-bottom lookout that hangs out over the edge! There is a small fee to go on the lookout. They plan to add a gondola, so you don't have to hike up, and a zip line to ride it down!

It might not be the most beautiful, but it is still one of the tallest functioning lighthouses in the world and the tallest in the Americas. The process of hiking up is exhausting for many, but for those that make it to the top, the view of the Pearl of the Pacific is breathtaking!!

Estero Del Yugo Eco-Preserve

An eco-preserve that is an excellent spot for a short hike while checking out the birds and the wildlife. The trails in the forest take you through lagoons where you will see crocodiles, so be careful! You have to pay to enter this reserve, and you can purchase affordable daily, weekly, and monthly passes. The Estero Del Eco-Preserve is located in Cerritos across the main street, Sabalo Cerritos, parallel to Playa Bruja.

Mazatlan Boardwalk

The Malecon goes to the historic center and Playa Olas Altas. Ocean view walks with sculptures along the way and a view of the three islands (Deer, Wolf, and Bird). Great for walking, running, and biking. From one end to the other and back, it's about 9.8 km.

Playa Olas Altas Boardwalk

Experience this 1.6-km out-and-back trail near Mazatlán, Sinaloa. Generally considered an easy route, it takes an average of 22 min to complete. This is a very popular area for birding, running, and walking, so you'll likely encounter other people while exploring.

You start your tour of this boardwalk in Mazatlan at the Monument to Pedro Infante, the famous singer born in 1917. You continue along Playa Olas Altas, considered the city's heart. You will come across the Carpa Olivera, a fascinating spa built on the sea in 1915 inspired by seawater pools in Lisbon. You finish your trip with the Monument to the Mazatleca Woman.

Isla de Venados

Discover this 2.3-km out-and-back trail near Mazatlán, Sinaloa. Generally considered an easy route, it takes an average of 47 min to complete. This is a popular trail for hiking, but you can still enjoy some solitude during quieter times of the day.

Isla de Venados is a small island located in the Bay of Mazatlán, across from the city of Mazatlán. It is a popular destination for practicing water sports such as kayaking, snorkeling, or simply resting. Since it does not have too much infrastructure, it is not one of the most visited.

The hike to the top starts from the beach and is quite easy at first. However, it starts to get steeper and with a lot of vegetation that usually blocks the trail.

Please note that De Venados Island is only accessible by boat, usually by sea kayak or speedboat.

Playa Punta del Sabalo

Explore this 6.1-km out-and-back trail near Mazatlán, Sinaloa. Generally considered an easy route, it takes an average of 1 h 19 min to complete. This is a popular trail for running and walking, but you can still enjoy solitude during the day.

Lovely walk along the fine sand beach with a lot to see and has several public accesses. The nice route begins at Playa Punta del Sabalo through the hotel zone. Ideal for watching the sunsets.

Playa Cerritos Sur – Norte

Head out on this 10.6-km out-and-back trail near Mazatlán, Sinaloa. Generally considered a moderately challenging route, it takes an average of 2 h 8 min to complete. This is a popular trail for running and walking, but you can still enjoy some solitude during quieter times.

Nice walk along the bike paths and the fine sand beach with a lot to see. Various public accesses to the beach. The quiet route begins near Playa Cerritos along Avenida Sábalo Cerritos. Perfect for seeing the impressive sunset.

Recorrido Mazatlan Sur

Experience this 6.4-km loop trail near Mazatlán, Sinaloa. Generally considered a moderately challenging route, it takes an average of 1 h 37 min to complete. This is a popular trail for running and walking, but you can still enjoy some solitude during quieter times of the day.

This enjoyable route explores many tourist landmarks in the southernmost part of Mazatlan. You start at the Monument to Pedro Infante, the famous singer, and son of this coastal city. You continue on the avenue along the sea with beautiful views of the Pacific Ocean. You will pass several viewpoints and cross the bridge to climb the hill to the Mazatlán lighthouse. Then, you loop back on the inland streets to your starting point.

Marina Mazatlan

Try this 18.8-km out-and-back trail near Mazatlán, Sinaloa. Generally considered an easy route, it takes an average of 3 h 57 min to complete. This trail is great for hiking and road biking, and you'll unlikely encounter many other people while exploring.

This is a great exploration of the heart of the city of Mazatlan! You start at the Plaza de Toros and go through the entire "Golden Zone" with several beaches and hotels. You can stop at Punta del Sabalo if you wish. It curves around the marina, where you can admire the boats and yachts. You end up at Playa Cerritos to lounge on the sand with sea views.

Playa Isla de la Piedra (Stone Island)

Head out on this 5.5-km out-and-back trail near Mazatlán, Sinaloa. Generally considered an easy route, it takes an average of 1 h 3 min to complete. This trail is great for bird watching, running, and walking, and you'll unlikely encounter many other people while exploring.

Just a little distance from the famous port and coastal destination of Mazatlan, Isla de la Piedra offers less crowded beaches but with all the beauty and services of the big city. Visitors to this beautiful beach can enjoy peaceful walks or runs while admiring the many palm trees that the region's coconut farmers grow in the area.

Monumento a Pedro Infante – Mirador la Marea

Explore this 1.9-km out-and-back trail near Mazatlán, Sinaloa. Generally considered an easy route, it takes an average of 30 min to complete. This trail is great for road biking, running, and walking, and you'll unlikely encounter many other people while exploring.

With this short and easy route, you will enjoy the beauty of this popular coastal city. You start at the monument to Pedro Infante, the actor and singer from the golden age of Mexican cinema and probably the most famous son of Mazatlan. You continue along the avenue heading south and climb the Cerro del Vigia for an unforgettable view of the city, the port, and the Pacific Ocean.

Emerald Bay – Playa Cerritos

Get to know this 2.9-km out-and-back trail near Mazatlán, Sinaloa. Generally considered an easy route, it takes an average of 39 min to complete. This trail is great for hiking and walking, and you'll unlikely encounter many other people while exploring.

The beautiful course begins at the Emerald Bay Hotel and will take you to Playa Cerritos through the hill. You will have an incredible view of the entire Pacific Ocean. Ideal to go for a walk at any time of the day and have endless walks. You will be delighted with the impressive sunsets over the sea that make the sky seem like a work of art.

Mazatlan Central Park

Get to know this 3.1-km out-and-back trail near Mazatlán, Sinaloa. Generally considered an easy route, it takes an average of 36 min to complete. This trail is great for walking, and you'll unlikely encounter many other people while exploring.

Mazatlan Central Park has beautiful lakes where you can rent kayaks, grassy spaces perfect for a picnic, shaded areas with trees, and many paved trails perfect for strolling, jogging, or running. It has an Environmental Ecological Center with indigenous flora of the region. It is a place suitable for the whole family.

Bike Riding In Mazatlan

Mazatlan has gone to great lengths for you to enjoy a nice bicycle ride in its beautiful city by installing modern bicycle lanes along the Malecon, Rafael Buelna, and Cerritos. These bike lanes are well lit at night so bicyclists can ride and enjoy the city day or night!

Mazatlan hosted the 2000 Mountain Biking World Cup, which put it on the map since it was the first time the world cup had ever been in Latin America.

Are you a mountain biker looking to take on some challenging single-track trails that take you up the Sierra Madre mountain range? Do you just want to chill, taking in the ocean views while riding on a cruiser bike along Malecon's new bike lane? Are you looking to participate in races or an all-day, long-distance tour? For every level of rider, Mazatlan is an awesome bike destination!

Mazatlan also hosts bike races, tours, and events throughout the year. The city even has a non-profit, Perros Sin Dueno, whose mission is the advancement of cycling in Mazatlan. They organize rides you can join every Sunday to meet new people and enjoy the great outdoors in Mazatlan.

There are plenty of bicycle shops to rent, buy or repair your bike, and most of these shops put on tours, and depending on your level of experience, there is a tour for you. Here is a list of the most popular shops in town that can get you on your adventure.

- Kelly's Bicycle Shop and Tours
- Bluefoot Tours & Expeditions

- Mazatlan Bike Tours
- Baikas Bike Rental and Segway Tours
- Epic Mountain Bike Riding

Mazatlan Fishing

Mazatlán is located on the west coast of Mexico, just outside the Gulf of California. This beautiful area has plenty of things to do to keep you busy while you visit, and fishing is one of them.

The fishing in the area is known to be great, emphasizing offshore fishing. Because it is so close to the Gulf of California, Mazatlán sees many fish migrating through its waters in the spring as the water warms up in the northern parts of the bay.

In Mazatlán, you can find plenty of inshore fish as well; while species are more limited compared to some areas, the species there are in large numbers. While most fishing is done in the ocean, many different saltwater lakes, marinas, and inlets are also available. No matter where in Mazatlán you go, you can be confident that you can find fish.

Deep Sea Fishing

Deep sea fishing is a big attraction here in Mazatlan for fishermen and women worldwide. They come because its waters are teeming with pacific sailfish and striped marlin in the winter, with the warmer summertime waters bringing massive blue and black marlin, giving it the name "billfish capital of the world." Dorados (Mahi Mahi), massive yellowfin tuna, and mako sharks are big catches in this area.

The best months for deep sea fishing are when the fish are more abundant and have an aggressive feeding activity from May to November.

The average price for a private 4-hour Mazatlan deep-sea fishing trip is around USD $350, while an 8-hour trip will run you over $500. These prices fluctuate with the season, but those are the current prices on fishingbooker.com for Pepe's Fleet 28' Sport Panga charter.

I have been fishing here in Mazatlan with Ron Heslop and getting on some good fishing trips!

Check out his Youtube Channel to see some great fishing. You'll see me catching a couple of Marlin!

Bottom Fishing

While not common knowledge in the fishing community, you can spend a fantastic day on the bottom water fishing here in Mazatlan. Large Snook, Snapper, Seabass, Grouper, and Pampano top the list. With the all-year availability of small to sizable live shrimp, the odds of catching these trophy fish are in your favor. To find out the current prices for bottom fishing and book a trip, fishingbooker.com can help.

Shore & Surf Fishing in Mazatlán

Mazatlán has some great shore and surf fishing across the city. From fishing in marinas and inlets to surf fishing from one of the many beaches, you'll be sure to find some fish.

If you are surf fishing, rigging a shrimp or baitfish with some weight and letting it drift along the bottom is a great way to catch various species.

If you are fishing in marinas or inlets, using moving baits is a great way to cover a lot of water. Some of the most sought species in these spots are snook and jack crevalle, but if you are surf fishing, you can expect to catch more of a mixed bag.

Best Fishing Spots-Surf / Shore Fishing

Estero La Escopama

Estero La Escopama is a large lake north of Mazatlán. This lake mainly offers triggerfish and jack crevalle. The lake is connected to the ocean, dumping into emerald bay. You can fish along the shoreline in quite a few areas.

The main reason why the lake is so good is because of how many little bays and inlets are in the lake. This gives the fish plenty of structure to hang around.

Another reason is the constant flow of baitfish into the lake. Seeing that the lake is connected to Emerald Bay, tons of bait fish swim into the lake for protection from the weather or predators in the bay's deeper water.

El Cid Marina Beach

This beach is located on Marina Mazatlán and offers great snook and jack crevalle fishing. There are areas within the marina where you cannot fish, but on the beaches, fishing is great.

A few different spots are scattered throughout the marina, but this spot is one of the most productive as it is located near the mouth of the marina.

Emerald Bay

Emerald Bay is located north of Mazatlán and holds plenty of inshore fish species, with the occasional offshore species passing through the area. In this bay, the main targets will be snook, snapper, grouper, and amberjack. Permit fishing in this area is also a very popular species.

Bass Fishing

Mazatlan is world-renowned for its incredible bass fishing. On **Lake El Salto,** monster bass, 10 pounds or more, fill this lake, and 30 to 80 catches a day are about the average! Lake El Salto has been featured in fishing magazines and television programs worldwide. With English-speaking representatives, Mazatlan Tours can get you fishing on this lake quickly. For more information on their packages, look at their website.

Lake Picachos, located 30 miles northeast of Mazatlan, is a clean freshwater bass haven. Significant numbers of 2 to 5-pound bass with a lake record of over 12 pounds.

Fishing is strictly catching and releasing, and it's not uncommon to catch 50 to 60 bass in a single afternoon. If you are a bass fisherman, you'll want to try your hand at these professional trips with Fish with Larry. They offer bass fishing packages on Lake Picachos; those details are here.

Do I Need a Fishing License In Mazatlan?

Yes and No. If you are taking a boat out to go fishing, you need one, and the cost is $15 a day. You can purchase one at the marina on the day of your trip. Fishing licenses are also available by week and month. A fishing license is not required for ocean fishing from the shoreline.

Historic Sites

Mazatlan was founded in 1531, and each of its historical landmarks has its own story, illuminating the culture and its history. Tourists have always been attracted to them due to their long, unfolding story, beauty, and breathtaking views.

Teatro Angela Peralta

It opened its doors on February 14th, 1874, becoming a majestic cultural and historical site considered the most important theater in northwest Mexico, where plays, dance, opera, and music are presented.

Cathedral

In the heart of the Historico Center is the Cathedral Basilica of the Immaculate Conception, built between 1875 and 1899, and is considered the most beautiful in northwest Mexico.

Centro Historico

It's the main spot for cultural life in Mazatlan, the ideal place for a family atmosphere, where joy, tradition, and culture are combined in the oldest part of the city.

Museo Pedro Infante

This museum has historical value in Mazatlan since it was precisely in this house that the idol of the "golden age" of Mexican cinema was born. Here you can admire the artist Pedro Infante's belongings.

Museo De Arte

Open space to express history and exhibit the most important works of art of internationally recognized Merican artists representing Mazatlan's heritage.

Palacio Municipal

Historic building in which dozens of mayors and councilors have decided the directions of the city. The Municipal Palace is not just a building. On its walls, you can 'breathe" stories of Mazatlan.

Museo Arqueologico

In the Archaeological Museum, you will discover part of Mazatlan's past by observing collections of archaeological pieces, artifacts, clothing, weapons, and symbols of the ancestors who inhabited these lands.

Casa Paredes O Herrasti

A majestic house built between 1904 and 1907 embellishes the Old Mazatlan area. It is one of the most valuable architectural constructions since it was one of the first residences in the port.

Outdoor Adventure and Beach Relaxation

Thanks to a recently renovated historic center and endless stretches of sandy shore, the coastal city magnetizes travelers with a penchant for outdoor adventure and beachside relaxation. At the top of all Mazatlan itineraries should be a cliff-diving show, during which visitors can watch fearless divers plunge into the Pacific Ocean from dizzying heights.

In Centro Historico, the likes of Plazuela Machado and Teatro Angela Peralta make for gorgeous walking tours. At the same time, in Zona Dorada (Golden Zone), Playa los Sabalos and Playa las Gaviotas swell with visitors soaking up year-round sunshine.

From the city, day trips to the foothills of the Sierra Madre Mountains for ATV rides and ziplining are popular for thrill-seekers.

Culture connoisseurs can gain insight into local culture during a tour of El Quelite. At the same time, Stone Island (Isla de la Piedra), home to coconut tree-fringed beaches and authentic Mexican restaurants, is a great place to escape for half a day.

Also within easy reach of Mazatlán is El Rosario, renowned for its artisan crafts; the Estero Ecological Reserve, home to more than 270 species of bird; and La Noria, where blue agave plantations and tequila distilleries abound.

So while you are here in Mazatlan, you can do plenty of things to enjoy your holiday. In this guide section, I will show you ways to do that through tours offered here. To do that, you can browse through the tours in this section, and if you see something you like, you can also book it through viator.com/tours or any other tour operator in the area.

Mazatlan Shore Excursion: Small Group Highlights Tour with Lunch

This small group tour will show why Mazatlan is a famous resort town popular for its sandy beaches, alluring nightlife, and tasty food. On our half-day 5-hour city tour, you will see the variety and cultural richness of this Sinaloan coast gem for yourself. You will enjoy the Spanish fort lookout hill for fantastic city views and the El Faro lighthouse at the top of the Cerro del Creston, famous for being the highest lighthouse in the Americas.

You will be stunned as we show the renowned cliff divers jumping into 8 feet of rock-laden water from high up. The jumps are off a 50-foot high platform, and the divers must time their jumps right to take advantage of the slightly higher water depth of the incoming waves; teamwork is needed where other divers will help each diver time their jump perfectly.

We then head into the Centro Historico district, or Old Mazatlan; you will feel like you stepped into the 1950s as you pass by grand homes, the downtown market, and the main plaza. This former pirate haven has undergone a resurgence in recent years as a blossoming artist and entrepreneurial hub.

Venture inside the beautiful Immaculate Conception basilica and take photos of this old church in Mexico, then drive to the Malecon (boardwalk) to the Golden Zone for the best shopping and beach areas. While here, enjoy an authentic Mexican lunch of mouthwatering shrimp or the famous Mazatlan fish filet, then shop to your heart's content or just relax on the beach and enjoy a refreshing swim before returning to the port. This half-day tour provides an excellent overview of the enchanting city of Mazatlan.

Whale Watching

Enjoy a seasonal tour that not all travelers experience during this half-day whale-watching excursion off the coast of Mazatlan. Ideal even for visitors with limited time in the region, you'll be able to spot a wealth of other marine life as you search for humpback whales, something you couldn't do independently.

- Go humpback whale-watching off the west coast of Mexico
- Look out for turtles, sea lions, dolphins, and more.
- Complimentary drinks are provided onboard
- The small group capped at 12 participants guarantees an intimate experience

Mazatlan 5-Hour Guided ATV Tour

Escape the bustle of Mazatlan on a guided ATV tour through the Sierra Madres. In addition to navigating the terrain, your guide offers background information on the landmarks and towns passed along the way. After a buffet lunch and tequila tasting in a small town near Mazatlan, enjoy free time to explore the local history museum and church. Round-trip transport is included for your convenience.

ATV's Tour to La Vinata Los Osuna and La Noria Pueblo Señorial

Their company´s owner´s family came from La Noria town, where they lived most of their life and constructed the Los Osuna distillery, which has given work to thousands of locals during most of the past 143 years. With them, you´ll experience a fantastic adventure and a historical experience.

Mazatlan Sightseeing and Beach All Inclusive

This is the best tour if you want to have all your daily activities, lunch, and drinks are taken care of. You will not have to worry about where to eat or what activities to do. You will have plenty of options at your hand to choose from. And your Tour Guide will always be with you for anything you need.

Sierra Madre Villages Half-Day Cultural Tour

Escape Mazatlan's bustle in favor of the rustic charm of Concordia and Copalia, colonial towns cradled by the Sierra Madre Mountains, on a 5-hour tour from Mazatlan. Visit 16th-century stone temples, admire the colonial architecture, and observe artisan crafts such as bread- and tile-making. Refreshments, hotel pickup, and drop-off in Mazatlan are included on this small-group tour, limited to 15 people.

Mazatlan Smart Bike Tour

Explore the historical sites in Mazatlan easily on this guided electric bike tour. Travel around the streets of the city's historical center, which aren't accessible via large tour buses.

See the Cathedral Basílica de la Immaculada Concepción and the El Faro Lighthouse, one of the highest lighthouses in the world. Plus, watch cliff divers plunge into the coastal waters.

- See the highlights of Mazatlan easily on this bike tour.
- This tour is suitable for those who need more time.
- Ideal for cruise ship passengers; the tour departs from the terminal.
- Choose from a morning or afternoon start time

Mazatlan Lighthouse (El Faro)

Situated on Cerro Crestón, Mazatlán's highest hill, formerly an island, El Faro, is visible from 30 nautical miles away. While day-trip boats to Stone Island often pass beneath Mazatlán Lighthouse, the natural appeal lies in seeing this landmark up close.

Hike the moderately challenging 300 steps to the top independently or visit the lighthouse during a half-day city tour. Both walking and biking options are available. When there, look out for the recently added glass-floored viewing platform.

Stone Island (Isla de la Piedra)

Stone Island is a common Mazatlán full or half-day trip destination, and many excursions to Isla de la Piedra include sightseeing tours of Mazatlán's Old Town. Ideal for time-pressed travelers that can see the El Faro lighthouse from the boat side.

Tours typically build in adventure activities, but independent travelers can arrange horseback riding, snorkeling, and even mangrove visits upon arrival to Stone Island.

Otherwise, Stone Island is great for collecting seashells, relaxing under palapas while enjoying fresh seafood, or sipping ice-cold beers in hammocks.

Ten Islands Expedition

Visit places that are tricky to get to alone during this half-day tour of some of Sinaloa's most important islands and islets. Look out for marine creatures you might not otherwise get to see, visit beaches many travelers miss and snap photos as your guide teaches you about the history and geology of each location.

- Visit several Sinaloa islands, beaches, rocks, and islets in just half a day
- Look out for gulls, frigates, ducks, dolphins, turtles, stingrays, and more
- Benefit from your guide's insight to learn about the locations and wildlife
- The small group capped at 12 participants ensures an intimate experience

Plazuela Machado

Sometimes known as Plaza Machado, Plazuela Machado has developed thanks to a donation of land from local businessman Juan Nepomuceno Machado. Highlights include the 19th-century wrought iron gazebo, which sits at the heart of the plaza, and the wide range of nearby old town attractions, restaurants, and events, such as book and food fairs.

Most city tours—whether walking, biking, or Segway- pass through or stop at Plazuela Machado and typically include further visits to the cathedral, Olas Altas Beach, and Ángela Peralta Theater.

Golden Zone (Zona Dorada)

Beginning at the intersection of Avenida del Mar and Avenida Rafael Buelna, the Mazatlán Golden Zone runs the length of Avenida Camarón Sábalo. Perhaps best known for large hotels and resorts, the Golden Zone is also home to some of Mazatlán's most attractive beaches and nightlife.

Half-day city tours include stops in the Golden Zone and typically offer free time to enjoy the beaches and water sports activities. If visiting independently, be sure to stop by the new Mazatlán Marina.

Old Mazatlan (Centro Historico)

Easily explored on foot in hours, Mazatlán Old Town is a walkable and historic district in this lively port city. Highlights include colorful and renovated French-inspired buildings, the central Plazuela Machado, a family-friendly square with live music in the evenings, and some small archaeological and art museums. Most walking, biking, and Segway tours of Mazatlán will pass through the Mazatlán Old Town and typically include stops in Plazuela Machado.

Olas Altas Beach (Playa Olas Altas)

Once a public pier, Olas Altas Beach and its ever-shifting sands are now popular among locals, first-time visitors to Mazatlán, and surfers. Make time to stop by the public Carpa Olivera swimming hole at the north end of the shore and stroll along the malecón (boardwalk), which runs the length of Playa Olas Altas.

Due to the proximity of Olas Altas Beach to Mazatlán Old Town, most city tours, whether on foot, Segway, or electric bicycle, tend to include at least a brief stop at the beach. These excursions typically include visits to other Mazatlán highlights, such as the cathedral and Plazuela Machado.

Angela Peralta Theater (Teatro Angela Peralta)

Not to be confused with the Mexico City amphitheater of the same name, the Angela Peralta Theater in Mazatlán was first inaugurated in 1874 and later restored and reopened in 1992. The theater is now home to a contemporary dance company, two small art galleries, and a cultural center.

Admire the theater's exterior during a guided city tour. Many biking and walking tours pass by the Angela Peralta Theater or visit independently to tour the interior or catch a show.

Mazatlan Aquarium (Acuario Mazatlán)

Across 34 saltwater tanks and 17 freshwater aquariums, visitors can admire a wealth of marine life at the Mazatlán Aquarium. Interactive highlights include shows featuring sea lions, tropical birds, and live feedings of nurse sharks and surgeon fish. Beyond underwater attractions, there are also walk-through aviaries and a crocodile lagoon. The Acuario de Mazatlán is the only aquarium in Latin America with a dedicated frog area.

Mazatlan Cruise Port

Mazatlan's exceptional beaches are its claim to fame, not just the touristy stretches of sand in town where you can surf, tan, or see the cliff divers. More adventurous travelers will find other, less crowded beaches accessible by taxi. It's also worth taking a guided walking tour of the historic city center.

You can learn more about the destination while visiting points of interest like Plazuela Machado and the Moorish-style basilica. Passengers looking for retail therapy can head to Mercado Pino Suarez for a selection of Mexican handicrafts or the Golden Zone for designer items.

Estero Del Yugo Nature Preserve

Established by Sandra Guido in 1997, Estero del Yugo Nature Preserve is a haven for birdwatchers in Mazatlán with a focus on conservation. Look out for species such as herons, egrets, roseate spoonbills, ibis, kingfishers, and more and other animals such as turtles, white-tailed deer, and foxes.

As well as walking nature trails, visitors can enjoy mountain biking, taking a boat ride through the estuary, and climbing the 12-meter observation tower independently or in the company of a local guide.

Old Town Mazatlan Segway Tour

The latest craze in modern traveling is undoubtedly a city tour by Segway. The easy-to-use Segway is a fun way to zip around Old Town and cover two centuries of its history that would otherwise be accessible on long, exhausting walking tours.

Hop aboard the self-balancing personal transportation device designed to operate in any pedestrian environment. Riding a Segway is intuitive and easy to learn. It's new, and it's cool and a ton of fun.

During this guided tour of Old Town and the waterfront, zip around landmarks such as the Plazuela Machado, the beautiful Cathedral, Olas Altas, and the Clavadista. You will explore Old Town Mazatlan from its modest beginnings to the vibrant city it is today.

You'll discover more with less effort and time with a Segway. This small-group tour is limited to six people, ensuring personalized attention and a guided Segway tour of Mazatlan—cruise through Old Town and the waterfront. Admire the city's architecture and watch daredevil divers leap off a cliff.

- Learn about the city's origins and evolution
- Choose from several departure times
- Small-group tour is limited to six people

Half-Day Ziplining Experience from Mazatlán

Add adrenaline to your Mazatlan itinerary with a zipline course that offers panoramic views rarely seen by visitors of the area's natural landscape. In addition to ensuring a comfortable and safe experience, your guide takes souvenir photos available for purchase after the tour. The day includes a traditional Mexican lunch, tequila tasting, and round-trip transport from the doorstep of your hotel.

Ziplines and Mezcal Tasting

Get your adrenaline pumping and feel the wind in your hair as you soar through the treetops on this adventure tour. Depart Mazatlan for the Huana Coa Adventure Park, where you can tackle a series of ziplines, platforms, a flex-walk bridge, and a nature walk.

Afterward, visit a local distillery to see how the famous mezcal liquor is made from start to finish. Enjoy tastings of local mezcal at the distillery. Get a bird's-eye view of the area on the ziplines. Hassle-free transfers from your hotel are included. All necessary equipment is provided for your safety

Sensation Bash Party All Inclusive Boat Cruise through Mazatlan Bay

Take friends and family on a tour of Mazatlan Bay on this fun boat experience. Put on your dancing shoes for the party while a live DJ takes care of the music. As you sail, you can also enjoy panoramic views of the city and the three islands in the bay.

The tour culminates with a beautiful sunset before returning to the dock.

- Enjoy drinks and dinner on board
- Meet other revelers as you cruise
- Relax in an informal setting
- See Mazatlan from a different perspective

Mercado Walking Food Tour

Taste your way through the Mazatlan market on a food tour that combines culture, history, and cuisine. You'll sample foods from tostadas to torta sandwiches and traditional Mexican ice creams, getting the real stories behind each flavorful dish.

Like the market, this tour is about more than food, and it's an inside take on the place where Mazatlan locals shop and socialize.

- The guided market tour features local cuisine.
- Enjoy seven expert-chosen food and drink tastings.
- Learn about the history of a fascinating Mazatlan neighborhood
- Convenient meeting point in central Mazatlan

Morning Tour All Inclusive Boat Cruise through Mazatlan Bay

It is a tour where Mazatlan is appreciated from a different perspective, and you can enjoy the sea through water activities accompanied by an open bar throughout the tour and an incredible party atmosphere. The perfect mix to make this a complete ride!

Mazatlan City Tour

This city tour of Mazatlán is a perfect introduction for first-time visitors and offers a good mix of history, scenic views, and free time. Drive along the boardwalk and watch professional cliff divers leap from 50-foot (15-meter) platforms.

In Old Mazatlán, see 19th-century landmarks like the Ángela Peralta Theater and Mazatlán Cathedral. You'll also have time for some souvenir shopping at a local market. Half-day Mazatlán city tour. Local guide. Good value for the money. Hotel pickup and drop-off included.

Barrio Bites Tour

Want to taste Mazatlan, soak up history, and pick up street food confidently? Ready to take your taste buds on a roll and find your inner flavor adventurer?

Mexican cuisine is practically synonymous with street food. But with so many food stands and carts, it's hard to know where to start. The Flavor Teller will take you to the best-hidden gems in

Mazatlan. Get off the beaten tourist track and experience authentic flavors on culinary backstreets.

Spice up your day and learn about Mexican culture through food. Satisfy your curiosity and appetite. Feel welcome at family-run food stands that create culinary magic and break through cultural and language barriers.

4-Hour Private Bird-Watching Tour in Mazatlan with Pickup

Knowing the beauty of a region through birds is a true privilege that cannot be missed. Mazatlan is rich in gastronomic culture, but above all, in its biological value, and they have birds that you will not find anywhere else in the world. We invite you to discover them through our eyes and our extensive knowledge.

Private Van and Bilingual Local Driver

Choose your itinerary (and your adventure) on this full-day, private, guided tour of the coastal region of Mazatlan. Nestled on the Pacific Coast and home to 13 miles (21 kilometers) of the beachfront boardwalk, this beautiful area is home to historical sites, architectural landmarks, seaside cliffs, lighthouses, and restaurants.

- Let your guides help you build the perfect day by the shore.
- Private tour to see what you want when you want
- Guide and driver to take you where you want to go in an SUV or van

- Tour Mazatlan and get a comprehensive introduction to the city

Bird Island

Isla de Pajaros is the northernmost island of the Reserva Ecológica Islas de Mazatlán, offering superb natural recreation. As the name hints, Isla de Pájaros (Bird Island) is a hotspot for our winged friends, part of a diverse ecosystem inhabited by more than 400 species.

To enjoy the island's wildlife, scenic beauty, and crystal waters, this tour provides a guide, kayaks, and snorkeling equipment. Enjoy Bird Island! Snorkel and kayak in a beautiful reserve area off the coast of Mazatlan. Visit a diverse ecosystem known for more than 400 species of birds, including the white-winged pijije, the red-billed rabijunco, and the brown heron.

A guide will ensure your safety, provide water and snacks and give information about the island's ecology and wildlife. All the equipment to get to the island and enjoy its nature is provided.

Day Pass at Mazatlan Beach Front Resort with Lunch

Get picked up from your ship and spend the day exploring the oceanside Golden Zone with this full-day access pass to a beachside resort. Soak in the hot tub, swim in the pool, lounge on the beach, or get active on a personal watercraft, kayak, or try high-flying parasailing.

Break for a drink and lunch of fresh seafood and explore the resort before being dropped off at your ship.

- Drive along the Golden Zone coast
- Full-day access to resort amenities and beach
- Pickup and drop off from your cruise ship
- Lunch and two beverages included

Kayak by the River

Venture off the beaten path of Mazatlan on a kayaking tour of the Presidio River. As you cruise down the river, your guide eliminates the stress of navigating unfamiliar territory alone.

After working up an appetite, enjoy a freshly-prepared lunch of regional cuisine. Options to visit hot springs or indulge in a tequila tasting are also available.

Hot Springs Pools

Enjoy an afternoon of restorative relaxation soaking in mineral hot springs. Enjoy at your door, pick up from your Mazatlan hotel, and get away from the tourist trail. The springs are rich in magnesium, calcium, sulfur, and carbon which work to alleviate aches and pains.

Some find a soak in the springs is also good for the skin. Afterward, there will be time for lunch and exploring the town.

- Regional Mexican lunch included: try tequila cheese and machaca burritos
- In town, visit the tequila museum and have a tequila tasting
- Remember to bring a swimsuit, towel, and pocket money for souvenirs

- Round-trip transportation from your hotel or cruise ship terminal included

City Tour & Mazatlan Lighthouse

There's more to Mazatlan than beaches alone, but the city's public transit system needs to be set up for tourists, and self-driving can be difficult. See more of this fascinating city on this small-group guided tour in less time.

You'll stop at the historic Mazatlan Lighthouse, which offers spectacular 360-degree views of islands, coast, and city, ideal for vacation snaps.

- See the sights of historic Mazatlan in a group of a maximum of 12
- Soak up gorgeous views from Cerro Creston and the Mazatlan Lighthouse
- Choice of departure times lets you plan your day and fit more in
- Skip the self-drive stress, includes 2-way transfers direct from most hotels

Temazcal Sweat Lodge and Tequila Tour

Combine two typical Mexican experiences on this convenient half-day guided tour: a traditional sweat lodge trip and a tequila tasting. Visit the temazcal, a pre-Hispanic sweat lodge, where a shaman hosts you for a mud and steam treatment.

Enjoy hotel pickup and drop-off, a traditional meal, a tequila tasting, and a trip to the Museum of History as part of this comprehensive outing.

- Visit a traditional, pre-Hispanic sweat lodge called a temazcal
- Relax in a mud bath and let a shaman guide your experience
- Several sample types of tequila and eat delicious regional cuisine
- Save time and enjoy convenient hotel pickup and drop-off

Mazatlan Sightseeing and Shopping Tour

Explore the resort town of Mazatlan on a small-group sightseeing tour with the hotel or port pickup, including drop-off. Wander around the Old Town and learn about the history and culture of this colonial city.

See highlights such as the cathedral, the Old Spanish Fort, and the cliff divers. Plus, visit the modern Golden Zone and the beaches. During the tour, you'll also have time to shop for souvenirs.

- See Mazatlan highlights, including the cathedral and the Old Spanish Fort
- Discover great shopping in the Old Town and on the boardwalk
- Bottled water is provided to help you stay hydrated in the heat
- Convenient hotel or port pickup and drop-off in Mazatlan included

Mazatlan City Tour and Observatory

Get to know Mazatlan's beautiful streets and history. Take a step into history on a funicular ride. Admire the greatness of the port from the top of the Cerro del Vigia, where you will live a trip to the past inside one of the oldest buildings in the city.

At the same time, we will share the pleasure of knowing traditions in the mezcal process. Also, you will be participating in conserving rescued birds to create a unique memory.

Private Van Tour or Transportation

They started their tour and transportation business in 2002 after fulfilling their tour guide course to satisfy the high standards of the tourist industry. Their packages are tailor-made for you, their customer. You won't regret hiring them!

This tour will give you a chance to customize your tour from the following highlights in Mazatlan:

HIGHLIGHTS OF MAZATLAN

- The Malecon (Promenade)
- Lookout Hill
- Ice Box Hill
- Devil's Cave
- Cliff's Divers
- Old Town
- Downtown
- Immaculate Conception Cathedral
- Flea Market

- Machado Square
- The Changueras (Shrimp Sellers)
- The Flowers Market
- Golden Zone
- Day Pass in a BEACH + HOTEL (No extra charge)
- Lunch Time (lunch not included)
- Shopping Time
- Old and New Marinas.
- Residential Area

These are all recommended highlights for you to customize your Private Tour.

Resources Page

I used many resources here in Mazatlan to put this guide together, and I want to thank you all. There are just too many for me to list here, but here are the ones I did some serious digging around in and, they are all worth your time to check out.

MazatlanVisit.com

MazatlanPacificPearl

Goatsontheroad.com

Mexicodave.com

Mazatlantoday.net

Mexperience.com

Traveloffpath.com

Internationalliving.com

Manufactured by Amazon.ca
Acheson, AB